Multiball
Contact

by Drew Batchelor

Multiball Contact
    Copyright © Drew Batchelor 2006

Published By:
    The Ministry of Manipulation
    London, UK
Web: www.MinistryofManipulation.com
Email: Book@ministryofmanipulation.com

Design and Illustration: Drew Batchelor
Photography: Dr Mithila Shafiq
Cover Photograph: Dan Gordon-Levitt

First Published 2007   1

Printed in the UK by: Bath Press Ltd

ISBN 13:   978-0-9554739-0-6
ISBN 10:   0-9554739-0-X
A C.I.P. catalogue record for this title is
available from the British Library.

Whilst the advice and information in this
book are believed to be true and accurate
at the date of going to press, neither the
author nor the publisher can accept any
legal responsibility or liability for any harm
or injury arising from the techniques and
advice described in this book.

Please send comments, corrections and
suggestions for future editions to:
Book@ministryofmanipulation.com

Contents

A fter a decade of training, teaching and a lot of experimenting with rolling, balancing, dropping and picking up balls. I decided to put what I teach in classes and workshops onto paper, and to produce this book.

A book that I wish I had been given 10 years ago, a book to help make it easier to learn Multiball Contact.

This guidebook has three sections: The Lessons, Multiball Inspiration and Appendices.

The 16 lessons teach a course on Multiball Contact. Each lesson will help you to learn a particular fundamental technique. The Inspiration section does not *teach* tricks, it shows what is possible, and explains how they are done.

There are many names for this thing we love to do:
- Ball Contact
- Dynamic Manipulation
- Contact Juggling
- Ball Manipulation
- Crystals or Crystal Juggling
- Sphereplay ™
- Dancing With a Ball
- Dance of the Spheres, or just
- Playing with Balls

In the London scene we usually call it 'Contact', and for me Contact is the art of making balls dance, a graceful, relaxing, mesmerising and beautiful art form.

For some, Contact is a way to earn a living as a performer. For others, it's a way to meditate, to relax, a way to find balance or flow, a way to heal themselves or understand themselves or a way to gain control of their bodies - to explore movement and dance. And for another crowd, it's a cool way to chill out with their mates. For some, it's a combination of the above!

Whichever is your preference, I hope you will find this book a comprehensive guide to Contact with 3 to 11 balls - everything you will need to know from absolute beginner to advanced Contact. Ball rolling delights such as palmspinning, pyramids, snakes, formations and morphing.

I also hope that with the lessons in this book you will enjoy the journey of learning Contact as much as I enjoy teaching it.

Drew Batchelor
The Ministry of Manipulation
www.MinistryofManipulation.com
London, October 2006

Which Balls to Use?

Getting the right balls will make the process of learning Contact much easier and quicker.

You will need 4 balls to work through the lessons in this book. If you haven't got any balls yet, take a look at Appendix 1: Balls and Appendix 2: Ball sizes. These explain all the different options for Contact and will help you choose the correct ball size for your hands.

Quick Answer

For the first three lessons you will need one ball. You can use an acrylic ball, or you could use a 75-100mm (3"-4") juggling stage ball (See Appendix 2).

For Lesson 4 you will need 2 smooth and slippery balls - acrylics or wooden balls. For Lessons 5 and onwards you will need 4 smooth and slippery balls.

Acrylic Balls

Best for Quality

Most contact jugglers use clear acrylic balls, usually referred to as "acrylics". Acrylics are beautiful, but they are also expensive. Fortunately if looked after, they will last a long time; mine are still in very good condition after 8 years.

- 70mm or 2.75": Cost £20, €22 or US$25 each.
- 75mm or 3": Cost £25, €34 or US$28 each. There is much variation. I've paid prices from £12-35 each.

See Appendix 1 and 2 for more information about acrylics.

Safety Warning

Sun + Acrylic Ball = Fire
Transparent balls can be dangerous. They are powerful lenses which focus the sun's rays and very quickly start fires that burn down houses and juggling shops. Always keep acrylics covered or out of direct sunlight when you are not using them. On a sunny day, you can light a fire or a cigarette in a few seconds and you will rapidly learn not to hold the ball stationary in the sun as it will quickly burn your hands.

Wooden Balls

Best Budget Option

Wooden balls make a good, cheap alternative to acrylics for all contact juggling. Softer, lighter, and with higher friction than acrylics, wooden balls make a lovely rich rubbing sound.

Wooden balls are available in 50-100mm (2"-4") sizes from juggling shops and from architectural model making suppliers. Unvarnished 75mm (3") balls cost around £5, €5 or US$5 each (see Appendix 1).

Lots of lovely acrylics

Often the first move learned in Multiball Contact is palmspinning 2 balls in one hand, the second move is 3 balls in one hand and so on.

But that's not the easiest path. Perhaps this is why Contact has in the past been described as very difficult to learn... It's not true.

Contact has been one of the untaught arts and has lacked well-developed teaching techniques or structure.

The 16 lessons presented in this book build up from complete beginner to advanced techniques. They will guide you through a simpler path to learning Multiball Contact, helping you develop good technique through the easiest method.

These lessons break down the learning process into a series of small stepping stones. None of the individual steps are very difficult, but they will take time and practice to perfect.

Repeat Each Lesson Several Times as Required

Don't expect to be able to do everything in every lesson first time. You will find that it is by repeatedly revising and polishing the lessons that you will gain the technique to progress with the multiball in the Inspiration section.

Mind Games in Lesson 8

If you are a Beginner to Multiball Contact

Work through the lessons in this book in order.

The first three lessons use 1 ball to explain some of the principles that underpin this course. By Lesson 4 you will be working on 4 ball Contact.

Each of the lessons takes about one hour, and some may need to be repeated many times until they are mastered.

Repeat each lesson as often as you need. Generally, the best students are those that spend time polishing their technique on the basics rather than jumping on to try to learn new "moves" too soon.

After 8 years of palmspinning I still practise many of these exercises as part of my warm up every time I play Contact.

See also the advice on Training Methods on page 77.

If You Already Have Experience of Multiball

The lessons aim to teach technique, not moves. They may pretend to teach moves, but each one was devised to help manipulators focus on an important piece of technique.

Even if you can already **do** a "trick", like 2 balls in one hand, I hope you will still gain from doing Lesson 4 (2 Balls in One Hand) and likewise with all the lessons. At least you may gain a new understanding of theory or a new method by which you can help teach others.

It is by polishing 2 ball palmspinning that you refine your control and technique enough to palmspin 5 balls in one hand.

How Long will it take to Learn Contact?

Contact is not a race. The slower you progress through the lessons, the better technique you will develop.

How well you progress will depend on how much time you have spent prasticing the basics.

Good Contact is not about whether or not you are *doing* a move. It is about how well you are doing that move.

Smoothness, style, technique and quality are key. These are the measures of true progress, rather than just adding another move to the list of tricks "you have learned how to do, but need to spend a lot of time to clean up".

I teach these lessons over six weeks, although many students spend longer perfecting them, especially the advanced exercises. It could take anything from six months to three years to learn to do these smoothly, consistently and with style.

Indexes

As well as a conventional Alphabetical Index of Tricks and Moves by **Name** (page 160), you will find a useful index by **Difficulty** (page 158) at the back of the book.

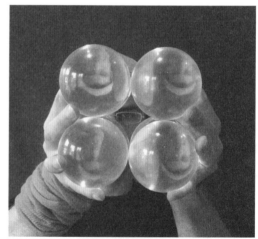

8 Ball Cube (page 120)

Difficulty

The moves in this book are rated from 1 to 5 on "The Super Ultimate Cosmic Contact Pyramids of Difficulty Scale ®©™":

It's not totally accurate, but it should give you some idea of how long it will take to learn each move and also whether you are ready to start working on a particular move.

Within the chapters in the Inspiration section moves are mostly arranged in increasing difficulty. The Index by Difficulty (page 158) should help you make a route map to work through the inspiration section.

You may find this scale to be way out of whack. If you find a move much harder than I have rated... sorry. There is some variation in how hard people find particular moves, and for many moves, the hand and ball sizes will have an effect on difficulty.

For more about difficulty see:
Appendix 3 - What is Difficulty?
To make things less difficult see:
Training Methods for Manipulators - page 77.

The Super Ultimate Cosmic Contact Pyramids of Difficulty Scale ®©™

	Rating	Moves
	1 Cosmic pyramid of difficulty. Good to learn for beginners.	Contact Tango (Lesson 1) Hamster walks (Lesson 2) One potato, two potato... (page 83) Holding a pyramid (Lesson 5)
	2 Pyramids - a little bit harder. It will take 1-2 hours to start to feel like you're "getting" it and a few weeks to become solid.	2 balls in one hand palmspin (Lesson 4) 3 ball triangle (page 84) 4 ball palmspinning- 2 in each hand Holding a line (Lesson 6)
	3 May take a few weeks to make good progress on these moves. Expect to be practising contact for several months before getting these solid.	3 in one hand palmspin (Lessons 11,12,13) 4 ball snakes (Lesson 9) 3 ball ratchet (page 85) 5 ball flat top rocket (page 102) 6 ball palmspin - 3 in each hand
	4 More advanced. These might take months or years to get clean.	4 balls in one hand palmspin (Lesson 15) 7 ball rolling W (page 113) 4 ball helical snakes (page 98) 8 balls palmspinning - 4 in each hand
	5 Cosmic Pyramids of Difficulty - Bleedin' Nora! That's difficult.	5 balls in one hand palmspin (page 96) Most 9, 10 & 11 ball contact Palmspin 3 in one hand separated (page 87) 4 ball helical train (page 100)

Warming Up...

If You Don't Warm Up...

Warming up for Contact is as much about preparing your mind as it is about preparing your body.

Contact is neither high impact, nor is it generally inherently damaging to the body. When done correctly, it can have lots of physical benefits.

Warming up can increase your awareness, improve co-ordination, reduce risk of injury, improve elasticity of muscles and give you greater efficiency of breathing.

Warming up will help you learn quicker and drop less.

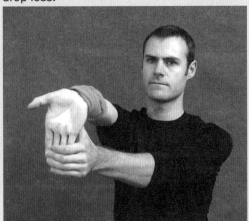

If you pick up your balls without warming up, you could find yourself frustratingly poor at contact for the first 15 minutes and not able to make moves consistently, even those you thought you had solid.

When cold, you are training your muscle memory to do the move badly, to over-react, and drop the balls. In this 15 minutes of un-warmed up "practice" you're not getting better at controlling contact, you are training your body to do it worse.

The most sure-fire way to become a better manipulator and juggler is to warm up, and cool down for every practice session. Sadly, to their loss, many manipulators and jugglers do no warm up and those that do, appear to average about 5 minutes.

Warm up to Prevent Injury

The three most serious kinds of injuries related to Multiball Contact are:

○ Strain or tension in the back or neck.
○ RSI (Repetitive Strain Injury) symptoms from excessive or un-warmed up multiball contact, or trying to progress too quickly or with too heavy balls.
○ Those caused by dropping heavy balls on things, people and puppies.

Warming up can help with 1 and 2. There are risks of RSI like injuries from any repetitive hand activity. If you start to get any discomfort or warning signs like repeated pain or aching in your hands, wrists or forearms, during or after practice, then take a break, cool down and consult a doctor.

Warm Up and Stretching for Multiball Contact

First, get your body and mind into a good state, and then start playing Contact. There are different kinds of warm ups for different kinds of activity. Good options for your warm up are a session of Tai Chi, Qi-Gong or Yoga. These will set you in a perfect mental state for Contact - relaxed and calm.

Warming up for a small Contact session, even if you do nothing else, do steps 1 and 4 (below); a few minutes of joint rotations followed by starting gently. I use the exercises in Lessons 1-4 as part of my warm up and as a revision of the basic material of Contact.

Before you start a long full-on Contact session of several hours, it's a good idea to warm up thoroughly, for a minimum 15 minutes. You could try the following:

1 Joint Rotation 2-5 Minutes

Working from your fingers down to your toes make slow circular movements at each joint clockwise and counter-clockwise until the joints move smoothly. This eases joint motion and reduces friction and damage in the joints by lubricating them with synovial fluid. You're not stretching them, you're just trying to get your joints to wake up.

Work from your fingers to your toes:
- Fingers and knuckles
- Wrists
- Elbows
- Neck & Shoulders
- Trunk and waist
- Hips
- Knees
- Ankles, and finally
- Wiggle your Toes.

2 Aerobic Activity 5 Minutes

Jump around, jog, play with a skipping rope - any activity to warm your body up a couple of degrees.

3 Light Stretching 5-10 Minutes

Light stretching starting with the neck and back, then shoulders, arms, hips and finally legs. Not heavy stretching as if you're trying to improve flexibility.

4 Start Gently 5-10 Minutes

The final stage is to start doing Contact gently. Practise a watered down version of the exercise that you will be doing. Don't try to learn anything new or to practise anything you can't do in these first few minutes.

...and Cooling Down

Light cooling down and stretching immediately following exercise will reduce tightness, muscle fatigue and soreness. Ideally, you should finish your practice or play sessions with a cool down.

This can be the same as your warm up, in the reverse order.

A minimum warm down from a light contact session would be a few minutes of joint rotations. A warm down from a long session could be:
- 10-15 minutes of light training to finish your session off, followed by,
- 10-15 minutes of light stretching, then
- Finish with joint rotations.

Cooling down plays an important part in preventing injury. It also makes you feel better the next day.

Useful Information, Anatomy & Diagrams

Anatomy of a Hand

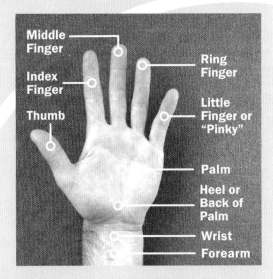

Middle Finger
Ring Finger
Index Finger
Little Finger or "Pinky"
Thumb
Palm
Heel or Back of Palm
Wrist
Forearm

Honestly, I don't think you're stupid, this anatomy diagram is for those who don't have English as their first language!

Exercise Heading & Lesson Duration

Lessons and exercises each have an estimated duration, for example:

Ex 5.4 4 Ball Rocket
15 min

These guidelines recommend how long you should spend on each exercise. These do not give you an estimate of how long it will take you to learn the exercise. Instead, these guidelines recognise that most beginners don't want to spend too long on any one single exercise. Additionally that beginners usually have not yet developed the strong finger muscles associated with Multiball Contact and so some exercises are limited by what is physically practical for a beginner without raising the risk of injury - tired muscles don't learn well.

Each full lesson is 45 - 60 minutes long as this is the optimum time for concentration without rest. It is intended that each lesson will be repeated several times, and may require many hours, weeks or months to master.

Sign Conventions

North, South, East & West
Some descriptions of moves refer to the directions, North, South, East and West. These assume that you are facing North, hence, West is to your left, East to your right, and South is backwards.

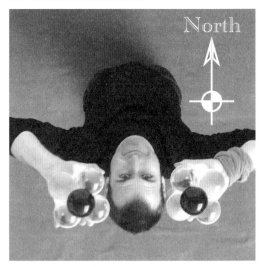

North

Inwards and Outwards
In palmspinning we refer to "inwards" and "outwards". Inwards rotation goes in across the front (as shown with the white arrows in the picture - right). Outwards rotation is the opposite and goes out across the front (black arrows).

Lines of Potential

Forwards & Reverse

In manipulation and juggling, every move has a pair - its own reverse. The reverse of a move is always the time-reverse of a move. It is what you would see if you made a video of a move, and played the video backwards. For example, inward palmspinning is the reverse of outward palmspinning (below).

Often the reverse of a move is also its mirror image, e.g. Exercise 5.4: Spinning a 4 ball rocket (page 36). Occasionally the reverse of a move is identical to it done forwards - it includes its own reverse. e.g. Exercise 2.1 Finger Waves (page 18).

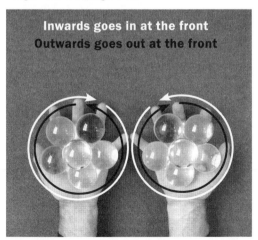

Inwards goes in at the front
Outwards goes out at the front

M any diagrams have either arrows or "Lines of potential". Arrows show either the movement of the balls, or the hands:

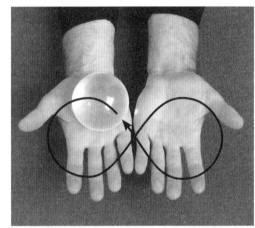

Roll the ball in an 8 shape on the palms

Some of the lines don't have heads, these are the "lines of potential". They indicate the flow of the motion without forcing it to go in only one direction. You can imagine lines around you, which show the potential future paths of the ball, then take the ball on a journey along one of these paths (Lesson 1 and Donny Darko Snakes page 94).

Any arrow in this book can also be read backwards. This will help you work out the reverse of a move.

Generally, the colour of the arrows doesn't have a meaning. White arrows are on a dark background and black arrows are on a light background.

Some rotational moves also indicate the axis of rotation as a dashed line:

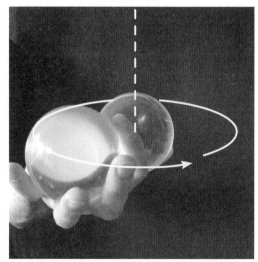

The axis of rotation is shown as a dashed line. The centre ball is stationary, the left ball is orbiting (from Mind Games, page 47).

Hand Positions

In Multiball Contact there are two common hand positions, which are called "the basket" and "the tray". They are shown in the pictures below.

Mirror Images

Most of the pictures in this book are intended to show a mirror image of your position. You may find it helpful to use a mirror to help you decode the images.

When left and right are written in the text, for example describing the tray picture below: This is the tray position, with the ball in the **left** hand, meaning **your** left hand, not mine.

Advanced Exercises

At the end of most lessons there is an "Advanced Exercise". The first time you try a lesson, you're not expected to be able to do these advanced exercises. Some of them are very difficult. Some even require you to have completed and polished the last lesson, Lesson 16, before you can attempt them!

Their aim is to give you new ideas and areas to explore when you come to repeat a lesson at a later date.

Morphing Notation

Many moves in the inspiration section have a number next to their title like this:

"Hourglass [3.1.3]"

This [3.1.3] is called "Morphing Notation". It describes the shapes of formations with lots of balls. It is explained in Appendix 4: Morphing Notation. (page 149)

The basket

The tray

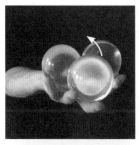

Multiball
Contact
The Lessons

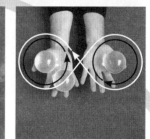

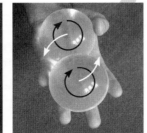
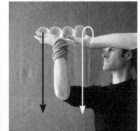

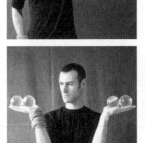
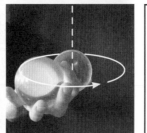

Master ball control
in just 16 lessons
with the Mr Myagi
school of Contact:
"Ah Danielson,
Wax On.
Wax Off."

Lesson 1: Contact Tango

Ex 1.1 Three Simple Holds

`4 min`

Welcome to the absolute first lesson for ball manipulators - it is simply about how to hold a ball. These first three lessons will ease you gently into 1 ball Contact before moving onto 2 balls in Lesson 4.

Duration: 50 minutes first time.
Ball: One 4" stage ball, or one 3" to 4" acrylic or even an orange is fine.
Level: Absolute beginners & good training for ball manipulators of all abilities.

In this lesson we use just three simple ways to hold a ball: on the palm, on the fingers and held in the fingers.

Try out these holds, focus on making clean shapes with your hand and present your fingers evenly spaced, as if you are offering the ball to an audience.

Relax! In Contact, you will never need to grip a ball tightly. Hold the ball with your hand as open, loose and relaxed as possible, so you are almost dropping the ball. Imagine you are holding a baby bird.

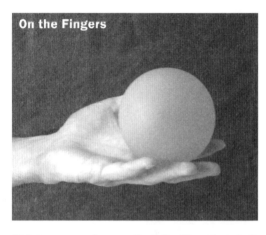

On the Fingers

This lesson works equally well with a stage ball (above) or an acrylic (below)

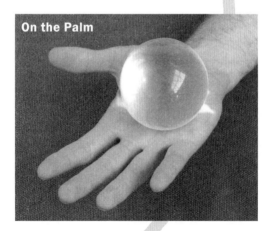

On the Palm

Held in the Fingers

Poses & Moving the Ball

10 min

For this lesson you can be sitting, but it is preferable to stand. If possible, listen to some relaxing, slow music while doing this exercise. The exercise is simply to move the ball through points in space, using only the three holds on the previous page. Try to keep with the tempo and mood of the music.

This may seem a bit crazy, but stick with it, there is method to this madness. This exercise will allow you to grasp what Contact should feel like.

Most beginners go too fast. Contact is NOT a race. The quickest learners I've seen are the beginners who take their time and try to move the slowest.

Match the movements to the music. If you don't have slow music, then make the movement fit your breathing. Make one movement (or one pose) for each in or out breath. Be aware of the expansion and contraction of your chest.

Making postures

The three pictures below should give you some inspiration: straight lines, circles or a 3D construct. Alternatively, imagine your own framework and move the ball around it.

There is no right or wrong in this exercise when it comes to when to move, where to move or how to move. Try to play with the ball for at least 10 minutes.

Linear

Circular

A 3D Grid in space

Ex 1.3 Journeys

6 min

The first exercises were about making postures. This exercise is to do the same thing with one little difference. This time instead of focusing on the postures, focus on making journeys - the paths between the postures. This subtle shift in thinking will change the feel of the exercise.

Imagine a path in space that runs around the whole room, take the ball on that journey. Again try also to match the mood of the music or to link those journeys with each breath.

Contact Commandments

The following are details that many beginners have difficulty with. These Contact Commandments apply to every lesson and trick in this book – to all your Contact, whether performing or not:

1 You don't need to keep doing things all the time. Stillness can be beautiful! Punctuate your Contact with pauses, commas and full stops.

2 Be aware of your whole body while playing Contact.

3 Don't forget your free hand (the empty hand). Keep it alive and involved in the action, it

should move as much and as often as the hand holding the ball. Also, make sure that you spend as much time with the ball in your left hand as your right.

4 Use your head! In Contact, movements of the head and eyes are as important as movements of the ball.

5 Staring intently at the ball is something beginners always do – acrylic balls are very beautiful. But you don't need to follow the ball with your eyes all the time.

6 You're presenting YOU, not the balls - don't hide behind the balls or 'doing a trick'.

7 If you enjoy practising Contact, let that show on your face - smile!

8 Always show as much of the ball as possible to your audience, don't let your hands block their view (unless you want to keep it concealed).

9 If you are standing up, you can move around. If you aren't into dancing (yet!), it may help to look at Tai Chi for inspiration. If you love dancing, then you'll find that almost any dance or form of movement can be slowed down and adapted to Contact, for example, Indian classical dance, Belly-dance, Yoga etc.

Ex 1.4 Two Handed Rolling

`10 min`

With your hands open and flat, hold a ball between your palms. There is only one rule in this game: Both hands must stay in contact with the ball, so it is held between your hands.

Move your hands. As you do, you will roll the ball around your hands, not just your palms. Also use your fingers, the backs of your hands, your wrists and your forearms to make contact with the ball.

To start with, keep your hands flat. Later, you can experiment with changing to different hand shapes, like the fists in the third picture.

Play! These pictures will give you some ideas to get you started - try to roll into and out of each of the following three positions.

Don't just keep the ball in one place, use this two handed tango to move it around like in the first two exercises.

Isolations

Isolations Kick Ass. In Contact they are any move which creates and illusion that the ball stays still, while what is supporting it is moving.

When I say "still" I mean completely frozen in space. Not wobbling a bit, but appearing to be perfectly stationary. It is this level of control that makes isolations difficult, and you need to put in hours of practice to polish them until they are perfect... and then you will realise that you can never reach perfection! This is why a really well isolated ball is something magical to watch.

Ex 1.5 Two Handed
10 min Isolations

With your hands open and flat, hold a ball between your palms and roll it around as if you were rolling plasticine or play-dough into a ball.

The ball stays still, both hands move in circles around the ball

Make your motions unhurried, and concentrate on keeping the ball REALLY stationary, with smooooooooth motion.

But that's easy, so let's make things a little bit harder. While maintaining the circular

motion of your hands, move the ball around like you did in the first two exercises - a moving isolation.

Next try different orientations. Instead of placing your hands on either side of the ball, try with one hand on top and one below, then swap hands while keeping the isolation tight throughout.

Isolations Explained

Isolated balls are not stationary. In a basic isolation the ball doesn't move anywhere (up/down, left/right or front/back) but the ball does still rotate - about its own centre.

A simple example to help understand an isolation is to imagine a unicycle on a treadmill. The wheel of the unicycle is still rolling forward, but it doesn't move anywhere.

In mechanics or physics you would say that Isolations rotate, but they do not translate.

" Tango is the glue that holds Contact together. "

Ex 1.6 Put it all Together - Contact Tango
15 min

Combine the first three exercises together, sometimes focusing on poses, sometimes on journeys, and sometimes incorporating holding the ball between two hands. If you aren't already, try standing up, and take your movements into three dimensions. Don't stay standing in one spot, move around - use these pictures for inspiration.

Take from this lesson four ideas:
- The slow and relaxed feeling of Contact.
- Contact can happen anywhere around your body, not just in front of you.
- A connection between your movement and either the music or your breathing.
- Contact is made with your whole body, including your head, eyes and empty hand, not just the hand with the ball.

More Contact Tango

Tango is the most simplified and pure form of Contact, I do it as part of my warm up every time I play. Practise your Tango regularly, play with it; give it your own flavour, character or personality. Every new move you learn, you can incorporate into your Tango, for example the 1 ball rolls in the following two lessons.

This is a simplified version of Contact Tango. A style of ball contact which can be developed much further, with more elements, concepts, isolations and techniques.

Lesson 2: Controlled Rolling

The next two lessons use 1 ball finger waves and palm rolling to explain a fundamental piece of technique - how to roll a ball.

This lesson introduces two concepts - two different methods for making a ball roll: the good way - *"controlled rolling"* and the not-so-good way - *"gravity rolling"*.

If you learn to make controlled rolls for every single roll you do, you will lay great foundations for ball Contact.

While gravity rolling might seem to bring progress at first, it's a bad habit that will cause problems with your technique later.

Duration: 50 minutes.
Ball: One 75mm-100mm/3-4" stage ball is ideal. Almost any ball will do; a 3" acrylic or an orange, but this is harder to learn with a small or light-weight ball.
Level: Absolute beginners, and it's also great training for ball manipulators of all abilities.

Ex 2.1 Finger Waves
15 min

Finger waves are a slow, smooth controlled roll made by rippling your fingers. The palms don't move at all, only the fingers and the ball move.

If just your fingers move, your audience will see a magical illusion that the ball is floating across your hands, with nothing propelling it. If you move your hands, the magic is lost.

Unfortunately, when you are creating an illusion like this, it is impossible for you to see it. Even a mirror doesn't help because you can't trick your own mind; It would be like trying to fool yourself with a magic trick. If you wish to see this illusion as performed by yourself, try using a video camera.

How to make a tray
To learn finger waves, first put your ball down for a moment and practise making a tray with your hands.

Make the hand position shown in the pictures to the right. Have the sides of your hands and little fingers touching and an even spacing between all your other fingers.

Try gently rippling your fingers without moving your hands. For presentation, lift the tray up to chest height and check that your shoulders are level.

Imagine rolling the ball
Practise rolling an imaginary ball on your fingers without moving the tray.

Slow motion with a ball
Now add the ball.
- Start by holding it between your thumb and your index finger.
- Slowly roll the ball across over the index finger - into the gap between your index and middle finger.
- Stop here and check that your hands are still level.
- Then roll to the next gap - between your middle and ring finger. Stop here and check again... etc.

So there are eight or nine positions in the gaps between your fingers.
- Move, stop, check.
- Move, stop, check.
- and so on...

Spend five minutes slowly moving the ball back and forth like this from one thumb to the other, using only movement in your fingers and thumbs and stopping in every position.

Smooth it out
Now get rid of the stops. Roll the ball in one motion from thumb to thumb as shown in the pictures to the left. The ball should be unhurried, it should take a few seconds to make this journey.

Not like this! Tipping my whole hand is "gravity rolling"

Try to lock your tray in position - your wrists and the palms of your hands shouldn't move at all. At first you will find this difficult to do without being tense, but it gets easier with practice.

Most beginners find it difficult to keep their hands in position. Either the weight of the ball coming into the hand makes it drop, or they try to lift the hand to tip the ball across to the other side. That would be "*gravity rolling*", what you need is "*controlled rolling.*"

If you find finger waves easy, you're probably not doing them right! Slow down and make sure your hands don't move at all, just your fingers.

Good finger waves create an illusion that there is nothing propelling the ball, that it is magically rolling along your hand. The less your fingers are moving, the more this illusion is enhanced.

This exercise it not quite as easy as it first looks, it's all about technique. The aim is not simply to roll the ball from one hand to the next. What is important is learning the skill to make the ball move smoothly and '*in control*', using only finger rippling.

Ex 2.2 Hamster Walking
12 min

Just like finger waves, hamster walking is all about rippling your fingers - "*controlled rolling*" not "*gravity rolling*" by 'pouring' the ball from one hand which has less control.

Practice exercise
Make the hand position shown (right) and ripple the ball forwards and backwards along the fingers of both hands without moving your wrists or palms.

Practise rolling the ball back and forth with either hand in front.

Hamster walking
Roll forwards into the front hand, then carry your empty hand from the back **underneath** to the front. It's a good style tip to carry the empty hand underneath so as not to obscure the view of the ball.

Try to go dead slow, imagine the ball is floating and make it smooth. Then gradually speed up to a slow leisurely pace, but at any speed remember to keep the rolling controlled, not through gravity.

Style tip

Lift your hamster walks and finger waves up to the height of your ribs. Hold your hands out away from your body and they will look a lot better.

Ex 2.3 Gravity Rolling - How Not to Roll
5 min

Gravity rolling is the way most newbies learn rolls in Contact.

So for this exercise, try to do some finger waves and hamster walks as badly as possible. See how many Contact Commandments you can break: bad posture, high speed, unrelaxed and jerky... you could even stick your tongue out to the side. Then, go back to trying to do them smoothly.

For your basic Contact rolling technique don't use gravity to move or stop the ball.

Not like this! Gravity rolling

Ex 2.4 Figure 8 & Palm Loops

18 min

Make a tray with your hands, identical to the finger waves exercise. Lock the tray in position. In this exercise the palms should move only a small amount to remove bumps from the path of the ball, your digits should do all the work, not gravity.

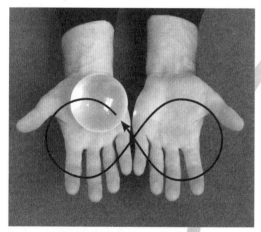

Cascade in a figure-8 shape

Cascade

First try a cascade, keep the speed of the ball slow and smooth, don't speed up or "chuck" the ball across the back of the palm. Done well, this will look and feel as if the ball is floating effortlessly around your hands.

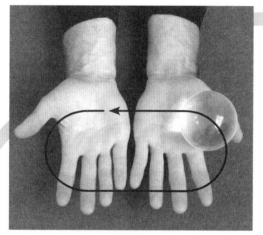

Loop - The tricky bit is the long roll across the back of the hands

Palm Loop

You will find loops a little more tricky than a cascade. Try to keep the long roll across the back of the palms slow. The ball only has to roll 10 to 15cm so it only requires a very gentle push with the thumb, not a hard chuck! This is controlled rolling.

Reverse

Try the reverse of loops and cascades. A reverse cascade comes forward across the middle. The reverse of palm loops clockwise, is the opposite direction - anti-clockwise.

It is possible to separately spin 2, 3, 4 and even 5 balls on the palms in this manner. In Lesson 14 you will return to this type of Contact.

Geeky Theory Stuff

If you've studied a bit of physics or mechanics, you might not be completely happy with the terminology of "gravity rolling" and "controlled rolling". After all, as manipulators living on this giant sphere, we are always working with gravity.

Even in controlled rolling, gravity is used to help move the ball. But the force of gravity does not dominate the movement.

If you want to progress with the minimum of effort and practice time, learn controlled rolling as your basic technique for all your Contact.

Later, as you progress, you should experiment with style, speed and gravity rolling. Then you could try creating rolls which are not pure controlled rolls or pure gravity rolls, but a combination of the two.

Lesson 3: Palm Rolling

Ex 3.1 Controlled Rolling Along the Palm
10 min

This exercise is a lot like finger waves, but instead of side to side, the ball will now go forwards and backwards along one palm.

Start position

1 Hold a ball so it sits on the heel of your hand. Press your fingers downwards to show the ball to the audience.

2 With minimal wrist movement downwards, move the ball to the dip in

your palm. Pause here and open your hand out to present the ball. Then on to (3)....

To move to each next position, make a slight dip in front of the ball and a slight ramp behind it. Make your hand movements as small as possible.

Keep going in little steps, move-stop-move-stop. You can make seven different stop positions along the length of your hand. When you get to your fingertips (7), reverse the motion and roll back 7, 6, 5, 4, 3, 2, 1, keeping the ball balanced and in control. At every point push your hand open and present the ball. Be aware of your posture.

Practise each hand separately, rolling back and forth from the fingertips to the heel of the hand. Stop in each of the seven

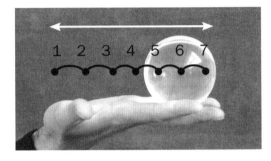

positions. When you feel that you have control in every position, gradually smooth it out, still maintaining an unhurried pace. Try to match the movement to your breathing, so the ball travels out on the out breath and back in over one inhalation.

If you are controlled rolling correctly, you will be able to stop the ball at any point in the roll and reverse it back to any point.

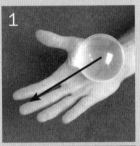

" Acrylic balls are magnetically attracted to cups of tea,
take care of your best china. - Official Contact Advisory Service "

Multiball Contact
LESSON 3: Palm Rolling

Ex 3.2 Zig-Zag
10 min Palm Roll Walks

Next practise the transfer between the hands. Combine this with previous exercise to create the whole move - Palm Roll Walks.

7 Starting with a ball on your fingers, roll it to your fingertips, the same as the end of the previous exercise. Stop it there, in control, later you will smooth out the stops.

8 Bring the side of your other hand into contact with the ball, near the back of the palm (shown right). Ease the ball across to the middle position (8), half on each hand.

9 Push slightly with the back fingers to bring the ball onto the heel of the front hand. Keep your hands flat so as not to obscure the view of the ball for your audience.

10 To make the release smooth, keep the ball in the contact with the fingertips for as long as possible.

From there roll along your palm to your finger tips and repeat this transfer starting on the other hand.

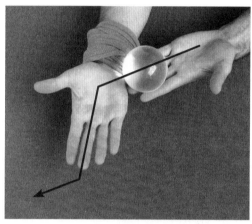

Zig-zag palm roll walks

Learn these walks using stop-motion, then smooth and slow controlled rolling. Later you can also experiment with speed.

You may start to find that the one breath per palm approach is a bit too tedious. So try experimenting with varying the speed.

There is no need to get these perfect, just yet. The following 2 exercises will give you plenty of practice.

Ex 3.3 Straight Palm Roll Walks
10 min

Repeat the previous exercise, this time transferring onto the back of the palm as shown below. This leads to a straight line palm walk, which is slightly more awkward, but visually more appealing.

Style point: Just like hamster walks, don't block the audience's view of the ball. After making the transfer, don't carry the empty hand over the top of the ball. It looks cleaner if you carry the empty hand underneath, or to the side, to bring it to the front.

It's very easy to get into a bad habit of hunching your shoulders while learning this move. Watch your posture and breathe.

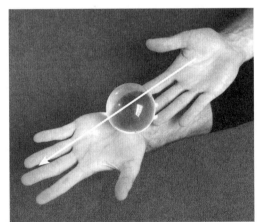

Harder straight transfer

Ex 3.4 Take a Ball for a Walk
10 min

Play with palm walks: forward, backwards and anywhere.

With practice you can palm walk anywhere, including high above your head, low to the ground and out to the sides. A great effect is to "take the ball for a walk", around your body and around the whole room or stage.

Incorporate hamster walks - a great movement is to start in a hamster walk, then gradually extend through a zig-zag walk and onto a straight palm roll walk. Slowly, return back to a zig-zag and finally finish in a hamster walk.

" Whenever you learn a new move, try to work out its reverse. This way, you will learn moves two at a time. "

Multiball Contact
LESSON 3: Palm Roll Walks

Ex 3.5 Reverse Lessons
10 min 2 & 3

The reverse of a trick is what it would look like if a video of it were watched backwards.

Reverse Hamster Walks roll towards you, as do reverse palm roll walks. The reverse of a finger wave is a finger wave, as they incorporate their own reverse.

For this exercise, go through Lessons 2 and 3 and make sure you have practised the reverse of all the exercises.

Beware. Sometimes, the reverse is harder than the forward move, occasionally a **lot** harder.

Ex 3.6 Combine lessons
15 min 1, 2 & 3

Put rolls, walks and isolations into your Tango. Take the ball for a walk, isolate it, hold it and move it on a grid in space.

It helps to have some music on and to stand up if you haven't already.

Adv Ex 3.7 Isolate Lessons 2 & 3

Hamster walks are good to isolate - if you can do these moves smoothly, you can make a perfect isolation. It looks great, and is one of the easier rolling isolation effects.

Palm walks are a little more difficult to isolate. The transfer between the hands can be difficult to get smooth.

Note: Palm Rolling Figure-8 and palm loops look incredible when isolated, but are very difficult to do with a clean isolation. They are actually an advanced version of Lesson 16 - palm circle isolations. It won't help your technique to spend time on it now, as there are far more interesting things to be doing...

...Time for Two Balls

That's as far as 1 ball goes in this book until Lesson 16 - 1 ball palm circle isolations. If you wish, you could try that lesson now, but be warned - it's not easy.

Time for a nice cuppa tea, then pick up another ball, turn the page and enter the world of palmspinning.

Lesson 4: Palmspinning 2 Balls in One Hand

This lesson will help you learn to palmspin 2 balls in one hand, with the balls always in contact with each other. It emphasises good technique which will make learning palmspinning with 3 or 4 balls in each hand an easier process.

Duration: 1 hour first time. You will need to repeat this lesson several times for it to become smooth and relaxed.
Balls: 2 acrylics or wooden balls. See page 138 "Which balls to use?".

Ex 4.1 Good Posture for
4 min Palmspinning

For all Contact, your posture is as important as what you do with your hands.

Most people practise palmspinning sitting on a soft floor: kneeling is best, while cross-legged is a good alternative. Do what's best for you. Before you begin, get comfortable - be relaxed and breathe.

Good Posture

Sit up: It's important not to slouch and to keep your back upright and straight. Slouching will damage your spine and give you a sore back and neck.

If you are sitting cross legged, tuck your ankles in before you drop an acrylic on them!

Hands up: Palmspinning looks more effortless at chest height than by your waist. Always keep a gap between your elbows and the side of your body. This stops you dropping one shoulder and breaking your posture.

Shoulders level: For this lesson, it may help to hold something in your free hand, preferably another one or two acrylic balls. This will help you resist the temptation to let the palmspinning shoulder drop, keeping you more balanced and centred.

Head up: This helps to stop you slouching. You can feel the balls, you don't need to look at them. If you find this makes it difficult to concentrate, try closing your eyes.

Good posture

Bad posture

Ugh. This feels dreadful. This will lead to a sore neck and back. Poor posture looks dreadful too. Be aware of presentation, even if you're not inclined to perform.

If you prefer the meditational side of Contact, opening up your posture will increase your awareness of your surroundings, not just the balls.

Bad Posture

Ex 4.2 Just Sit & Hold Them
5 min

First, hold 2 balls in one hand and just breathe and relax. Make sure the 2 balls are at the same level, don't let the front ball drop.

Use your free hand to rotate the balls to another position, side by side, or one in front of the other. Check the balls are level, hold them and breathe. Try this for a few minutes in either hand.

Good - level

Bad - tipped down

Ex 4.3 Gaining Control in
5 min Your Palm

Your thumb can pull or push a ball into the back of the palm, and the little finger can do the same.

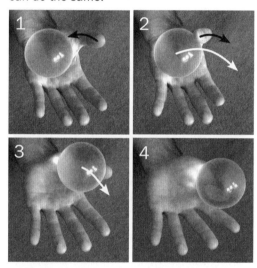

Put one ball down and place the other ball in the middle of your palm. Keep your hand open and relaxed.

With your thumb, reach over the top of the ball (1) and pull the ball out to the side along your thumb (2, 3 & 4). Then roll the ball back to your palm in the starting position, and open out your hand. Repeat this a few times in both hands.

Ex 4.4 Rocking

12 min

The second half of this exercise is gaining control with your little finger.

Starting with the ball in your palm.

(1) Reach up with your little finger and ring finger.

(2) Use these fingers to pull the ball and roll it out to the tip of your little finger (3 & 4).

Then roll it back to your palm and repeat these exercises with both hands until they becomes relaxed and smooth.

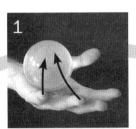
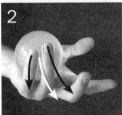
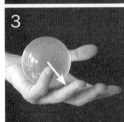
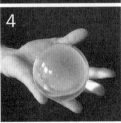

Hold 2 balls in one hand, make sure they are level (the front ball should not be lower than the back ball), and check your posture.

Simply start rocking the balls from side to side, moving about a quarter of a turn. Keep it slow and smooth.

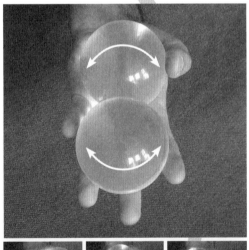

Repeat this with the balls starting side by side. Feel the balls in every position and don't be in a hurry. If you take things slowly, you'll get all you need from this exercise in 5 to 10 minutes. for each hand

Repeat this with both hands until it becomes relaxed and smooth.

Ex **4.5** Start Making Circles
15 min

Now extend the rocking motion, until it becomes half a rotation in each direction, then more and more until you finally start to **slowly** turn the balls continuously one way.

Everyone has one direction that feels easier at first, with 2 ball palmspinning it's not good training to just favour your good hand in the easier direction. Try to practise both hands in both directions and they will all become easy. See "Inwards or outwards" box on page 54.

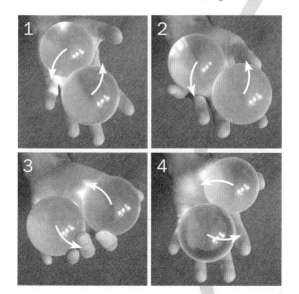

Palmspinning Super Hints

Aim for no clicks
In most palmspinning, the balls hitting together and making clicking sounds is a mistake. It can be considered as bad as dropping - it breaks the flow of the movement. This is palmspinning with the balls **always** in contact with each other.

You will learn this technique in less time if you are very strict with yourself about these two points: go very slowly and no clicking.

Keep the balls level
Be careful to keep the 2 balls level, don't let the front ball drop. Most beginners lower the front ball to some degree. Tipping the front down is easier at the moment, but it's a bad habit that will take a long time to unlearn when you start working with palmspinning pyramids (Lesson 15).

Free hand
Hold something in your free hand, preferably another acrylic. This will help to keep your focus more open, and to keep your shoulders level and relaxed. In palmspinning, always be aware of your posture and breathing. This is very important to your technique for making circles.

Make space
Don't try to push the balls around the circle. Instead make a space, a dip in front of each ball, for them to roll into.

Counter rotation
You may feel that the balls are slightly counter rotating in the direction of the black arrows. This counter-rotation is in the opposite direction to the way they are palmspinning (white arrows). Allow this counter-rotation and perhaps even encourage it and your palmspinning will be smoother.

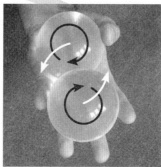

Slow and smooth
Keep a constant tempo: slow down the fast bits and avoid the tendency for the balls to speed up across the fingers. There are no lumps in the balls, all the lumps are in your hands!

Relax
Don't try too hard! Effort will not help here, your muscles need to relax into the motion. Palmspinning will not work well if you are tense in your fingers, arms, shoulders, neck or back.

And....
Practise in both directions and with both hands!

Ex 4.6 Shut Your Eyes and
5 min **Feel 1 Ball**

Place 2 balls in one hand. Check your posture, shut your eyes and breathe. Now slowly palmspin and focus **entirely** on your contact with **one** of the balls. Feel that you are stroking it as it goes around. There should be no position where you impede it and no position where you shove it, no jerks and no lumps, just smoooooooooth.

This exercise will smooth out the motion of the ball as it flows round your hand.

Ex 4.7 Shut Your Eyes and
10 min **Feel 1 Position**

Again with 2 balls in your hand. Shut your eyes, breathe, and as you palmspin, focus all your attention entirely on just **one point** on your hand.

Start with the pad at the base of your thumb. Feel each ball in turn as it makes contact with that point. It's a bit like a cat rubbing itself past you.

At first that point has no ball, so no weight on it. Feel the way that the pressure on that point gradually increases until the full weight of the ball rests there. Then smoothly decreases back to zero as the ball rolls away from the point.

Do this for a minute or so, then move your attention to the next position around your hand, for example the joint at the base of your thumb, and repeat the exercise.

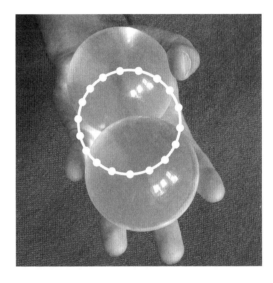

I can stop and feel the ball in 18 different positions in a circle around my hand (above) and practice this exercise focusing on each of those 18 positions.

This exercise is working to smooth out every part of the path of the ball as it flows around your hand.

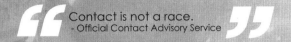
Ex **4.8** Ultra-Slow Ninja
15 min **Palmspinning**

Practise palmspinning really, really, REALLY slowly, one orbit of your hand every one to two minutes.

The balls will be almost stationary, but they should not stop, nor jerk forwards. Aim for a constant very slow speed, all round the circle. Take time to feel every position.

This will revolutionise your palmspinning, with a very small amount of practice. Do it for as long as you can manage, most people can take somewhere between two and fifteen minutes.

Afterwards, try doing some palmspinning at a more normal speed and you will feel a vast improvement.

Now you might understand better that Contact is not a race.

Adv Ex **4.9** Stand Up

Stand up and style it out. Don't just hold your hands in one position in front of you. Move your hands around while you are palmspinning, out to the sides, up and down. Experiment with different positions.

If you're not ready to palmspin with both hands at the same time - you don't need to yet; one hand can spin while the other is holding. Try incorporating Tai-Chi movements and positions while palmspinning. If you don't know any Tai-Chi, fake it!

Lesson 5: Holding a Pyramid

Ex 5.1 Holding a Pyramid
10 min

Jumping straight from 2 balls to 4 balls may seem a bit crazy, but have faith, more balls is not always more difficult. If you can spin 2 balls in either direction in either hand (and it doesn't have to be smooth) you are ready to start this lesson.

Duration: 45 minutes - 1 hour.
Balls: 4 acrylics or wooden balls.
To make this easier: Try taking 1 ball away - this lesson can be practised with 3 balls. Or use balls which are lighter and more rubbery than acrylics - like stageballs or satsumas.

Sit comfortably with good posture and relax your shoulders. Hold your hand out in front of you, palm up and keep a small gap between your elbow and your body. Your hand should be in its perfectly relaxed position - slightly cupped.

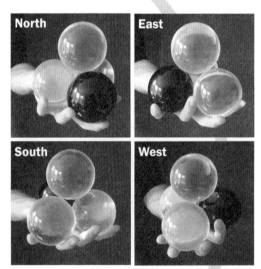

Holding a pyramid in different orientations

Place 3 balls in one hand in a triangle. Make sure they are all touching and don't grip the balls tightly. The position you want is slightly opened out from your relaxed, empty hand position. This will help prevent the balls

escaping out from the back of your palm. Gently place the fourth ball on top to form a pyramid.

Practise holding the pyramid with one ball pointing in different orientations: North-East-South-West. For reference here I have shown the black ball as the point. Use your free hand to rotate the pyramid around.

In each position make sure that all the balls are touching, and open out your fingers as much as possible and present the pyramid.

Repeat this holding exercise in each hand, until it becomes comfortable and easy.

Ex 5.2 Tipping a Pyramid
10 min Between Hands

This is the simplest method for transferring a pyramid between your hands.

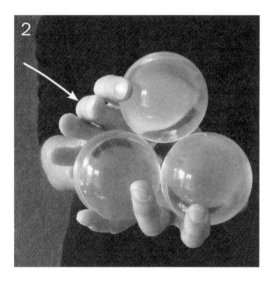

1 Start holding a pyramid in your right hand.

2 With your left hand, take hold of one other face of the pyramid.

Drat, a bad time to have to turn the page, sorry. Continued overleaf...

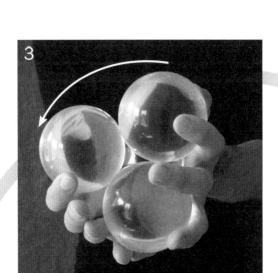

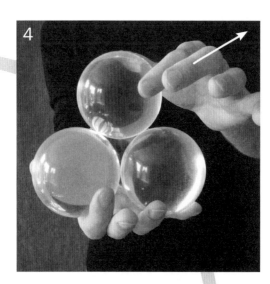

This transfer can be made on any of the three sides of the pyramid. Tipping forwards is definitely the hardest.

Practise this transfer on all three sides of the pyramid until it becomes comfortable and easy to keep all 4 balls staying in contact throughout the move, with no clicking together.

3 Tip it across onto your left hand. First, make the left hand take control of the side face - 3 balls, as one object. Then, as you tip it over, your right hand lifts, and remains in control of just 1 ball - the one that will become the new top ball.

4 Once you have tipped the pyramid into your left hand, check that all the balls are touching, THEN smoothly release the top ball from your right fingers. This method will make your transfers much cleaner.

Ex 5.3 Melting & Reforming a Pyramid
10 min

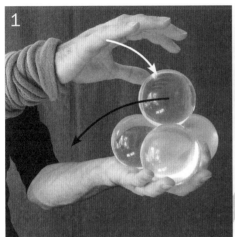

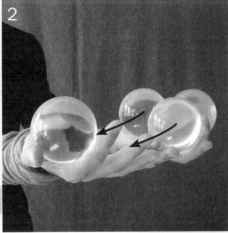

3 Check that the new triangle of balls in your left hand is horizontal and all 3 balls are touching. Then smoothly place ball 4 on top to complete the pyramid.

4 Repeat this in either direction until it feels comfortable.

This simple exercise helps you learn the skills to make and separate pyramids.

1 Start with a pyramid in your right hand. Take off the top ball with your left hand.

2 Simply pass the second and third balls across between your hands.

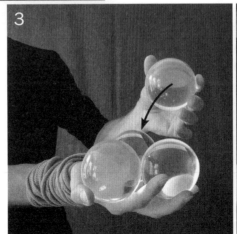

Ex 5.4 4 Ball Rocket

15 min

A 4 ball Rocket is the simplest way to spin a pyramid of 4 balls. Use your fingers to rotate the top 3 balls.

Hands in the basket position

As well as vertically (shown above), this can be done horizontally out to the front. To give this move a beginning and an end, put it in the middle of the transfers that you learned in exercise 5.2.

Don't just hold it still, funk it up by moving it around while you are turning it.

Ex 5.5 4 Ball Tango

15 min

This exercise is simply pyramid Tango, repeating Exercises 1.2, 1.3 and 1.4 (pages 13-15), using 4 balls as one object. Take it easy, you don't need to move quickly with 4 balls.

WARNING: Be careful when lifting acrylic or other hard balls above your head or other breakable body parts or objects.

Hold your pyramid up, move it around and transfer it between hands. In Tango, you can only hold a pyramid "on your palm", not "held in your fingers" like 1 ball, but you can hold it in 4 orientations, north, south, east and west in each palm.

In each new position make sure the balls are all touching and you have a relaxed posture. It's very easy to forget this and tense up with the weight of 4 balls.

The aim here is to learn to move pyramids around without dropping them, and to hold and transfer them between hands in many different positions.

If you find this too difficult, practise with 3 balls first. Then when you feel comfortable, add the fourth ball on top.

Later, you will find other movements you can add into your 4 ball Tango, for example, the curls in Lesson 7.

This is a lesson in learning how to hold and manipulate 4 balls in a line. They are just like the snakes in Lesson 9, only they don't wiggle.

"Look, matey, I know a dead snake when I see one, and I'm looking at one right now."

"No, no, he's not dead. He's restin'! Remarkable snake, the Norwegian Blue, Beautiful plumage!" *

(This was never said in The Dead Snake Sketch by Monty Python's Flying Circus)

Duration: 1 hour first time.
Balls: 4.
Get Ready: Working with lines and snakes requires 2 ball palmspinning skills. After warming up, revise 2 balls in one hand palmspinning (Lesson 4). You need to be able to rotate 2 balls in both hands in both directions, before starting this lesson.

Ex 6.1 Introducing Dead
20 min Snakes

Practise holding 4 balls as a line in different positions around your body and moving between these positions.

Holding in front
Touching little fingers together, present the line to your audience.

Holding in front

Dead Snakes Superhint I

Making a clean line
In each dead snake position, beginners often have a step in their line between the second and third ball (between the two hands). Work hard to get rid of this. It's this level of attention to detail that is needed to make snakes clean. This is what makes them difficult, it's well worth the effort.

Ball Contact is mostly done by feel. If you try to make your line clean by sight alone, your dead snakes will be scrappy. So here's the easy way – do it by touch:

Reach across from one hand to the other, either consciously touching the other hand, or touching the balls of the other hand. Train your hands to feel when the balls are in a straight line.

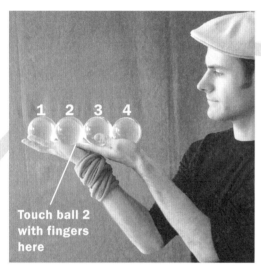

Touch ball 2 with fingers here

Holding to the side

Holding to the side

From holding in front, move your hands to the side. You will have to palmspin with both hands to make this position.

When you arrive at the side position, feel that the line is straight by reaching across with 2 fingers of the inside hand, to touch the second ball of the snake (Superhint I).

Dead Snakes Superhint II

To make this easier, think of the 4 balls as one object and move your hands around that object - the snake.

If you find this lesson too difficult, then try these exercises with something which *really is* one object. Use something your fingers can slide over, like an empty plastic bottle or a cardboard kitchen roll tube.

Good training for dead snakes

Alternatively, try using only 3 balls; 2 in one hand, 1 in the other.

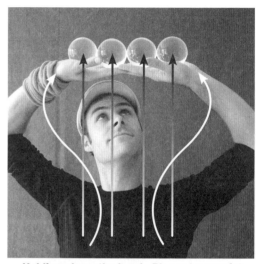

Holding above the head - Please be careful when you lift acrylics above your head

Holding above the head

First try holding in this position. Then try with a bottle, changing from holding in front to holding above your head. Start by bringing the inside of your wrists to touch while keeping the 4 balls in a line. Continue the motion with both hands turning outwards three-quarters of a rotation and lifting while palmspinning inwards to keep the line straight. (See "zeroing" in curls on page 44).

Roll down

A more complex transfer changing between holding above the head and holding at the side.

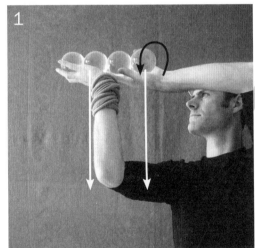

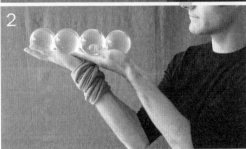

Start above your head, and move to your right. Palmspin your left hand to form the position shown in picture 1.

With your right hand grasp both balls. While isolating them, rotate your left wrist up over the top of the balls (black arrow). Then lower (white arrows) into the holding to the side position (2).

The 4 balls should stay in a straight horizontal line throughout the movement. Practise this in both directions on both sides, then experiment with combining it with the previous movements.

Style Hint

Dead snakes often look far more interesting if one of the balls is used to form a pivot for the movement. In the twist to vertical, we're using the back ball as a pivot, keeping it fixed - isolated in space as we change from horizontal to vertical.

Starting holding to the side, the easiest way to twist the whole snake up to vertical is to grasp all 4 balls and rotate the snake around the back ball (ball 4 in the "holding to the side" picture opposite).

When you get to vertical, rotate your hands around to the back to show as much of the balls to your audience as possible. Reach up with the index and middle finger of the bottom hand to touch the second ball and ensure a straight line (Superhint I).

Twist to vertical

Ex 6.3 Pyramid Melt to Line

`10 min`

H ere is a very simple way to connect between your snakes and your pyramids (steps 1-4 picture below).

By reversing this motion you can transfer from a line to a pyramid. Practise transferring into and out of a pyramid in each hand.

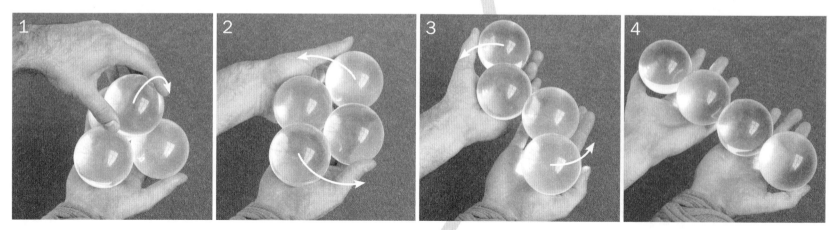

Ex 6.4 Dead Snake Tango

15 min

Make Contact Tango using 4 balls in a line. Out to the sides, above your head or low to the ground. Move gently between positions and in each position make sure your posture is good, your shoulders are relaxed and that the 4 balls make a clean line.

Try to explore all the potential of where you can move a dead snake, get very three dimensional - high, low, out to the sides (be careful when lifting acrylics above your head).

For the moment, keep your snakes on a grid, either perfectly horizontal, or vertical. This gives you and your audience a framework with which to understand their movement. Later when you have them in control, you can explore more organic paths.

Dead Snake Tango is my favourite title in this book. I'm charmed by the mental image of a smartly dressed gentleman dancing Tango with a rigor mortis frozen snake.

Adv Ex 6.5 More 4 Ball Tango

Build on the previous exercises and include two extra movements: twisting snakes to vertical, and changing between pyramids and 4 balls in a line.

Get creative and explore what you can do with 4 balls; as a dead snake, a pyramid and split into palmspinning 2 pairs. This is 4 ball Tango with all of Lessons 4, 5 and 6.

Soon, Lessons 7, 8 and 9 will extend your 4 ball vocabulary even further.

Lesson 7: Curls

Curls are a classic movement in manipulation and are seen in many of the ancient dances including Indian and belly dancing. They are really simple and look great.

Flashy waiters and cocktail flair bartenders perform this trick with a tray full of drinks.

Curls with 1 ball in each hand are very simple. The aim for this lesson is for you to get curls with 2 balls in one hand while palmspinning. Later you may wish to work on curling 2 balls in each hand at the same time.

Curls while holding 3 balls in each hand, without palmspinning, are not too difficult. Holding 4 balls is harder - don't expect to be doing it today. Curls with 4 balls in each hand while palmspinning is one the hardest palmspinning tricks.

Duration: 45 minutes first time.
Level: Absolute beginners and it's also great training for ball manipulators of all abilities. This is one of the easier multiball lessons.

Ex 7.1 One Handed Curls
10 min

See pictures 1-8 on opposite page. These curls are pictured with a 4 ball pyramid, but don't try that just yet. First, learn curls holding 1 ball in each hand. Avoid being tense, try to stay as relaxed as possible.

Experiment with the curling movement:
- Try doing it outwards as shown in the pictures and the reverse - inwards.
- Make the motion as small as possible, so the balls hardly move.
- Then try making huge curls, from the floor up to the ceiling, and as wide as possible. Include your whole body in the movement.
- Next, fix the ball in space - an isolation, then make the curling motion around it.

Try these all with the other hand.

Finally, repeat the above exercises holding 2 balls in each hand. Focus on keeping the 2 balls horizontal (so that later you will be able to palmspin them).

Be very careful at the top of the movement, you don't want to drop a heavy acrylic on your head or your toes.

Ex 7.3 Both Hands Curling at Once
15 min

Same again with both hands at the same time, 1 ball in each hand.

Explore these three options:
Mirroring: The hands form a mirror image of each other, so they both move outwards and upwards together.

Parallel: Both hands move as if connected by an invisible rod. They both move upwards and right together. Start with one hand in position 1, and the other in position 5.

Alternating: Curl having one hand going up while the other is moving down. There are many alternatives with two hands. Try starting one hand in position 1, and the other in position 4.

Then try to find the reverse of each motion you make and experiment with the small, big and isolated options from the first exercise.

Repeat with 2 balls in each hand. Try to keep both hands horizontal whilst curling, you may find this confusing at first.

Illustrations for Ex 7.1 One Handed Curls

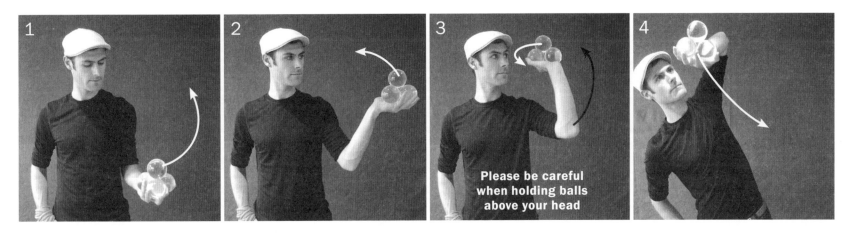

Please be careful
when holding balls
above your head

Light arrows show movements of balls, dark arrows show elbow movements. Learn these motions while holding 1 ball first, then while holding 2, then palmspinning 2 balls. Later you can return to this lesson and repeat it with 3 and 4 ball curls.

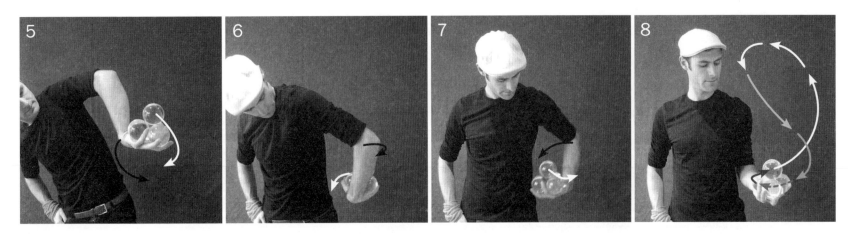

Ex 7.3 Learn to Palmspin in Many Positions
20 min

As a preparation for Palmspinning Curls practise palmspinning in many different positions around your body:
- Above your shoulder
- Behind your back
- Arms straight out to the side
- All seven positions shown on the previous page. Positions 4, 5 & 6 are fairly horrible to do. I find position 3 very relaxing and often play with it as an alternative to position 1.

Focus on keeping your palmspin level, oops!

Ex 7.4 Palmspinning While Curling
15 min

If you can palmspin 2 balls in all the positions of a curl, then palmspinning curls are within your grasp.

First time you do this exercise, focus on one curl - learning to palmspin outwards whilst curling outwards (try both hands, but not at the same time... yet).

If you find a lock - a place where one ball always falls off - go back to the previous exercise and practise that position until you gain the control you need there.

Whilst curling outwards with one hand, there are three different ways you can palmspin:
- **Outwards** - rotating with the curl,
- **Inwards** - counter-rotating to the direction of the curl.
- **Zeroing** - a funky visual effect where you palmspin the balls one rotation inwards whilst completing one curl outwards. Done correctly, the balls stay in the same east-west orientation throughout the motion. It's a form of isolation and as such, can be difficult to do cleanly.

With Palmspinning Curls, pay close attention to keeping the balls level. Smooth palmspinning with relaxed shoulders, neck and arms is what you are aiming for, and remember to breathe!

Curl Progression

Repeat this lesson several times. When you feel ready, practise with 2 balls in **each** hand. It may take you several weeks or months to get all the combinations of two-handed curls solid.

You can also repeat exercises 7.1 and 7.2 whilst holding 3 balls in a triangle or 4 balls in a pyramid (Tip: Use a stage ball for the top of the pyramid at first, it's going to fall off and it's less painful this way).

After completing Lesson 12 you can repeat this lesson with 3 balls in one hand, which is considerably harder. In a year or two you may wish to start working on palmspinning curls with a 4 ball pyramid. These are very difficult (Level 5). See page 117.

Adv Ex 7.5   Curling Dead Snakes

Curl a dead snake. This is an advanced exercise, not because it's a difficult movement to do, but because it is confusing to understand - especially when learning from a series of photos. Good luck!

The photos and hints for curling a dead snake are on the following page. The photos split the motion into two halves, going up and going back down. The halves should be blended into one seamless movement.

The first time you try this, you may find that it helps to use a plastic bottle, instead of 4 balls, to help you decode the motion. As you did in Lesson 5 with Dead Snakes.

This motion is useful for a lot of multiball manipulations. Many formations can be curled using this or similar movements. For example the 8 ball Torpedo (page 118) can be curled.

This is not the only way to curl a snake! The first of the Helical Snakes in the Helical Snakes Workshop (page 96) is also a two-handed curl.

Curl Power

The most important concept to take away from this lesson is not the curls themselves, but the practice of palmspinning in many positions (Exercise 7.3) and being able to move around and between those positions while palmspinning.

... Ex 7.5 Curling Dead Snakes Continued

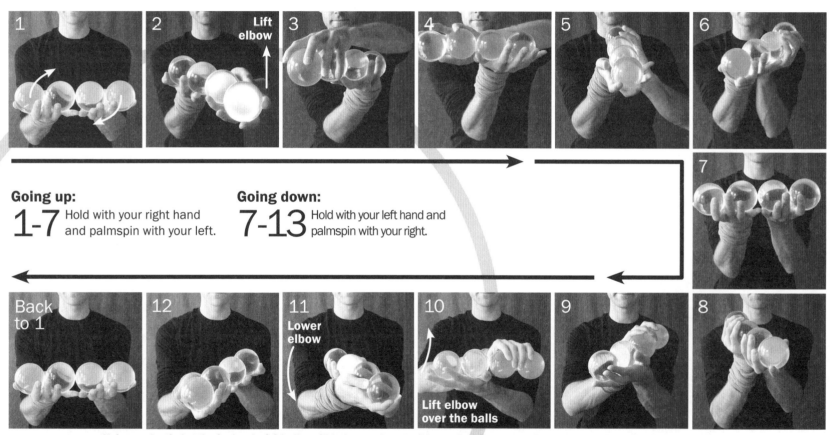

Going up:
1-7 Hold with your right hand and palmspin with your left.

Going down:
7-13 Hold with your left hand and palmspin with your right.

Using a plastic bottle, instead of 4 balls, will help you decode this motion. Treat the pictures as a mirror for your movement, your curled dead snake should always rotate anti-clockwise (going both up and down).

Ex 8.1 Isolated Palmspinning
20 min — **2 Balls in One Hand**

Mind Games is a name for all the great patterns that can be created by playing with 2 balls in each hand.

These are based on the 2 ball palmspinning that forms Lesson 4 (page 26). Usually they have bucket loads of isolated palmspinning thrown into the mix.

Mind Games can be played with the balls always touching their partner, or being separated (Lesson 10 page 56). I prefer the feeling of 2 ball palmspinning separated although, I first learned Mind Games, palmspinning with the 2 balls touching.

> **Duration:** 45 minutes first time.
> **Ball:** 4 acrylics or wooden balls.
> **You will need:** Solid 2 ball palmspinning in both directions and in both hands.

To learn 2 ball palm isolations, first make a mental picture that the isolated ball is fixed in space and your hand is moving around it.

You need to practise hard to get your isolated palmspinning in each hand to move with a smooth constant tempo around each circle. This is where all the extra effort you put in to make your palmspinning slow and smooth will bring rich dividends.

It is much easier to make palmspinning isolations with 2 balls, than the 1 ball palm circle isolations taught in Lesson 16 - which is essentially the same exercise, with the orbiting ball, missing.

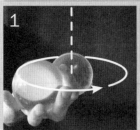

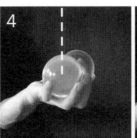

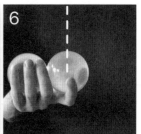

Exploring Mind Games

There are very few *moves* in Mind Games. There are, however, themes and ldeas to be played with. Practise each of the ideas presented here individually, until you feel you're starting to gain control of the balls.

Next, play with combining two ideas together. Create, explore and experiment. Practise each in several positions around your body and try to find new ways to change between them.

Try to make a continuous flow, from one movement to the next and to the next. Add a third idea, then a fourth. There are hours, weeks, months and years worth of great material to explore.

It helps to create a mental image that the 4 balls are one object. This mental image, is of one object that is changing shape, developing tension, flow and movement. Not an image of two or four independent objects. Even though they are not touching, the two pairs of balls are connected: by their rhythm, their movement and by you.

Alternating

Make a mental connection between one ball in each hand (dashed line below). Here the two centre balls are "connected", with one held just above the other, both are isolated.

The two outer balls are in orbit. The tricky bit is learning to isolate both hands at the same time.

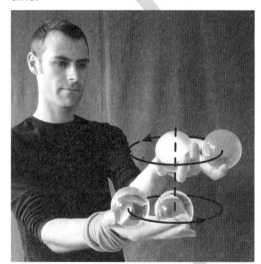

Alternating

By stopping one hand for half a rotation you can change to Syncro...

Syncro

Hold one hand just above the other, and keep the balls in the top hand directly above the bottom balls. Experiment with moving this Mind Game to different places, lift it up to head height or out to the left or right. Also, mid-flow, try swapping which pair of balls are isolated.

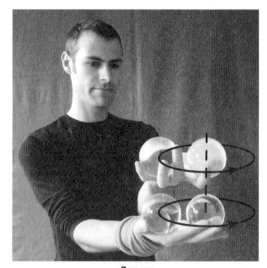

Syncro

Now try Syncro but with your hands palmspinning in opposite directions, one clockwise and one anti-clockwise.

Rails

Make 2 balls in each hand move around the space as if they are on rails. Palmspin to keep the balls either parallel to the rails, or perpendicular to the rails.

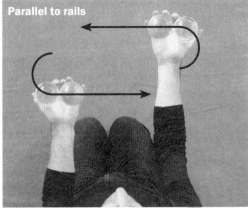

Parallel to rails

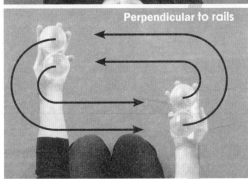

Perpendicular to rails

More Ideas:

- Each hand mirroring the other (above).
- Each hand orbiting around the other - think of the solar system.
- Moving three of the balls around the isolated fourth ball
- Add Dead Snake Tango from Lesson 6

Play!

Mind Games are a form of 4 ball Contact Tango. Imagine paths and structures in your mind, then take the balls on those journeys.

Mind Games will give you many ways to connect all the other 4 ball tricks: Dead Snakes, Live Snakes and pyramids. See the 4 ball Inspiration section for even more ideas.

Adv Ex 8.3 Confusing Polyrhythms

This one is a very nice headache. Palmspin one hand at twice the speed of the other. One rotation with your left hand for every two rotations with your right.

When you think you've mastered that, try three in the right and two in the left. This is an advanced exercise!

Lesson 9: Snakes

Snakes use 4 balls to create a character, an animated creature - good Snakes look awesome.

Snakes are a difficult movement to learn to do well, they require precise control of the balls. The following method should help you get some solid progress within a couple of hours.

Before starting to learn Snakes, you need a smooth control of:
- Lesson 4: Palmspinning 2 balls in One Hand (both directions, both hands)
- Lesson 6: Dead Snakes
- Lesson 8: Mind Games

Lesson Duration: 40min first time.
Be prepared to invest a few weeks or even months, to get them really clean and well presented. It will be worth it.
Balls: 4 acrylics or similar smooth and slippery balls.

Ex 9.1 How to Learn Snakes
15 min

1 Start in this position: In each of the positions shown, there are 3 balls in a line and 1 offset.

Focus on making this 3 ball line clean and straight. Beginners usually have a step in their line between the second and third ball (where their hands meet). Work hard to get rid of this. This level of control is required to make snakes clean, and it's this that makes them difficult!

2 Move your left hand slightly to the left and move your right hand to the right.

Keep the four balls in contact with their neighbours, with no clicking.

> Snakes: pay particular attention to the back ball, it's often lazy, ruining the whole snaky effect. - Official Contact Advisory Service

3 Palmspin both hands a quarter turn (both inwards) to make this shape, the mirror image of the starting position.

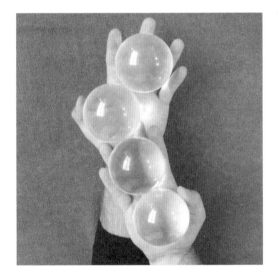

Check that all 4 balls are still flat (all 4 balls are at the same height when viewed from the side).

4 Move your left hand to the right and your right hand to the left.

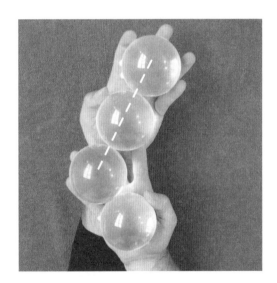

Keep all the balls in contact and make sure the 3 balls at the front make a clean straight line.

5 Palmspin the balls in both hands about one quarter turn and you should be back to the start position (below).

51

6 Practise the previous four movements until your muscle memory can make each of the positions very cleanly. This may take a while - a couple of hours or even a few days, if you have high standards. But first time, just practise for another 15 minutes.

Don't try to smooth it out yet... that will come in the next 2 steps.

Ex 9.2 Making These into
20 min Smooth Snakes

7 First, you need to minimise the size of the movements, so they are half those shown in the previous pictures. Like this:

More Snakes

If you want to learn more Snakes, you'll find 2 whole chapters on Snakes in the Inspiration section, including the advanced Helical Snakes Workshop.

Polish these micro movements. Again, this should take a while, but first time round just give it 10 minutes, then move on to step 8.

8 Then to make the snake, start blending steps 1 to 5 into each other. Step 3 should start before step 2 has finished and so on. This will become your smooth Snake.

Adv Ex 9.3 Snakes Everywhere

S nakes become a lot more interesting when they move around. Stand up and experiment with moving them all around your body and around the room.

When you think you can DO snakes, and you want a challenge, try this: repeat "Lesson 6 - Dead Snakes" and this time, bring your snake to life in every position and animate it, so it snakes between each position.

Palmspinning Superhints

Palmspinning is the most fundamental technique of Multiball Contact. It has its origin in the spinning of Chinese 'Therapy Balls' - small chiming metal balls also known as Baoding balls, which can be traced back to the Ming Dynasty (1368-1644).

This chapter gives superhints that apply to all palmspinning. Mastering palmspinning will take a lot of time, but this is a good thing. The journey to perfecting palmspinning is very relaxing, and palmspinning is a simple way to incorporate meditation into your Contact.

Superhint 1: Polish the Basics

Master palmspinners will tell you that your technique with the advanced moves will always benefit from reviewing and smoothing out the basics. See lesson 4 especially the superhints box on page 29.

Don't be in a hurry to pick up another ball, if you spend more time practising good technique with two, you will find it easier to develop control skills with 3 and 4 balls in one hand, and later even 5, 6, 7 and more balls.

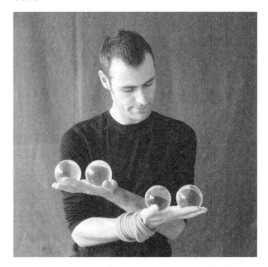

Superhint 2: Take care of Your Hands

Palmspinning can be very beneficial to your Hand Health, but not if you push it too hard. When you are first learning palmspinning, it is normal to find it quite tiring for your hands and forearms - the muscles in your forearms are the ones which control your fingers.

Ball manipulators who do a lot of multiball work get very strong fingers and toned forearm muscles. As you practise multiball more, your fingers develop greater control and you become stronger, so palmspinning becomes effortless.

Superhint 3: Don't Mindlessly Grind in Front of the TV

Absent-minded grinding your balls while watching TV is not practising to improve your technique, it's just teaching your muscle memory to do things badly.

It is better to concentrate on doing the exercises as precisely and carefully as you can. A few hours spent concentrated refining technique will give you far more control than dozens or even hundreds of hours spent mindlessly driving balls around your hands.

Perhaps later, when your technique has become more refined, then practising subconsciously, and playing while you're being distracted by the TV, may be productive. But be sure to regularly tune in your conscious mind to act as a subtle critic, checking and correcting your technique.

Superhint 4: Smooth & Slow

Always, right from the very first time you start palmspinning, aim to be click free and smooth.

Even if that means going really, REALLY slowly. This will save you months of training and considerably improve the quality of your palm circles.

Contact juggling is not a race. You're going to send a couple of balls in a circle, what do you want to be in a hurry for?

Inwards or Outwards?

Which direction is easiest?
Most beginners find rolling inwards easier because of the extra control from the thumb pushing the balls across the back of the hand. Often, as a palmspinner trains more, they start to find it less effort to spin rolling outwards because the thumb has less work to do.

Nowadays, because I've practised it more, I find palmspinning easiest anti-clockwise in both hands! That's rolling OUTWARDS in my left and rolling INWARDS in my right. This may be related to the Coriolis effect, because I am in the northern hemisphere!*

You will find the easiest direction is the one you train the most. Practise both directions with both hands, until they all become effortless.

*This sentence is not true.

" If you can hold it, you can turn it. "
- John Plastic

Multiball Contact
Palmspinning Superhints

Superhint 5: Every Click is a Mistake

Palmspinning feels and looks so much smoother when it is silent. A little bit of the 'energy' is lost every time the balls click together.

Good Contact is about developing control, while these random clicks as the balls hit together are a sign of a lack of control.

I've watched students achieve amazing results by learning palmspinning while dedicatedly focused on making sure the balls don't click together at all. They gained as much control with 2-3 weeks, training as I did with one year of practice.

However, if after learning to control palmspinning silently, you decide you want the balls to click apart and together, that's fine, it's a matter of taste. Some people even love to listen to the sound of their acrylics clicking together.

But, for learning palmspinning and as your "basic technique" aim for no clicks on your palmspinning.

Internal Energy

A purely physical or mechanical approach to palmspinning is to move the balls by pushing them around with your fingers - this seems to be the most obvious way.

But the physical approach is not the best technique; the internal method is to make space for the balls to roll into. Some would talk of Energy, Qi or Chi, flow or focus.

The technique presented in the lessons in this book will help you understand and develop these internal methods of Contact by feel and personal experience.

For those who wish to understand more about this, I recommend that you read further discussions of Tao & Taoism, Buddhism and internal martial arts including: Tai Chi and Qigong and in modern western psychology, discussions of "flow".

For those who wish to work towards developing these internal methods... Pick up some balls and turn over the page.

Lesson 10: Palmspinning 2 Balls Separated

Some ball manipulators prefer to palmspin with all the balls touching. Others favour palmspinning separated. Each has its benefits, for 2 balls in each hand, it's very useful to learn both techniques.

Separated palmspinning 2 balls in one hand often feels smoother than palmspinning with the balls touching.

Duration: 45 minutes.
Balls: 2 - almost anything slightly round.
Prerequisites: You are ready to try this if you have polished Lesson 4 - Palmspinning 2 balls in one hand (touching) in each direction.

High Friction Balls - No Problem

Separated palmspinning allows you to play Multiball Contact with all kinds of balls with either a sticky or slippery surface. Perfect for spinning silicone balls, stage balls and especially oranges.

Separated palmspinning is also smoother for manipulation with 3 and 4 balls in two hands where the balls are changing hands often, for example Lesson 14: 3 balls in two hands.

Separated technique permits palmspinning this pyramid of four sticky 100mm stage balls

Ex 10.1 2 Balls in One Hand
25 min Separated

To learn separated palmspinning repeat all the exercises from Lesson 4: 2 Balls in One Hand (touching), only with the balls held apart.

In Exercise 4.2 you learned how to hold the balls. This time repeat that, but hold them apart in each position. Then repeat 4.4 rocking, again this time separated, then starting to spin them, slowly and controlled holding the balls apart using your fingers, not using centrifugal forces.

Ideally the gap between the balls should stay absolutely constant, they should never click together. The gap depends on the size of the balls and the size of your hands, 10mm to 15mm is a good average gap.

As you speed up you will feel the balls being pulled outwards by the spinning action - the centrifugal force. Learning to spin separated and **slowly** will give you the control needed to make this trick clean at any speed.

As always, both hands and both directions!

Ex 10.2 More Separated
20 min Palmspinning

R epeat Lesson 8: Mind Games with separated palmspinning. This will help you get your 2 ball separated palmspinning far more solid.

Separated Mind Games

Super Hint:

Controlled Rolling
The wrong way to learn this trick is to try to spin the balls fast so they are pulled to the outside by centrifugal forces – this would be like gravity rolling.

Gravity rolling may feel like it is speeding your progress at first, but in the long term, you will learn quicker if you slow down and use controlled rolling technique.

3 Balls in Two Hands

Lesson 14: 3 Balls in Two Hands Separated (page 66) follows directly on from this lesson and uses separated palmspinning between two hands to create beautiful visual effects. If you like separated palmspinning, you can start Lesson 14 now and return to the 3 ball in one hand techniques in Lesson 11, 12 and 13 later.

Lesson 11: Preparation for 3 Balls in One Hand

How to Learn 3 in One Hand

Learning to palmspin 3 balls in one hand is a lot more work than learning to palmspin 2 balls in one hand.

This lesson will split the big step from 2 to 3 balls into lots of little stepping stones, helping to make the progression easier.

Duration: 45 minutes first time. Should be repeated several times.
Balls: 3 acrylics or similar.

This lesson and the following two lessons, are really three parts of the same lesson. Indeed many manipulators find that thumb and pinky-lifts (Lesson 13) are easier than palmspinning 3 balls (Lesson 12).

You will probably make the quickest progress if you practise all three lessons at the same time.

Ex 11.1 Revise Lesson 4:

15 min 2 Balls in One Hand

After stretching, complete your warm up by revising Lesson 4 for about 15 minutes.

There are a lot of good palmspinning technique tips in Lesson 4 which apply equally to 3 balls as much as they do to 2 balls. A quick revision of that lesson, focusing on the details of the technique will put them fresh in your mind.

When revising, you should try the first two exercises (4.1 and 4.2), holding 3 balls instead of 2.

Ex 11.2 Making Space with 2 Balls in One Hand
10 min

This exercise helps to make extra space in your hand. While palmspinning 2 balls in one hand, try to move the balls forward onto your fingers and spin them there for a few minutes.

○ Now move the balls backwards a little closer to your wrist than normal and spin them there for a while.
○ Next, move them towards the little finger side of your hand and spin there.
○ Finally move the 2 balls towards your thumb and spin there until it feels comfortable.

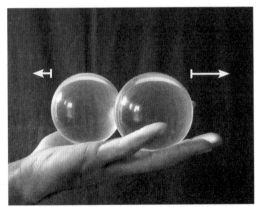

How far forward onto your fingers or backward towards your wrist can you move your 2 ball palmspin?

Ex 11.3 Learn 2 Balls in One Hand Separated
10 min

Polish the previous lesson. Practising your 2 ball palmspin separated until it feels natural and relaxed will also help to give you a feeling that you have more space in your hand by extending the area in your palm where you have control.

Again, helping to create more space in you palm ready for 3 balls

Ex 11.4 Revise Lesson 5: Pyramid Holding
10 min

Practise holding a 4 ball pyramid - it is better practice than trying to hold 3 balls flat. This is because holding a pyramid trains your hands to hold the base of the pyramid flat. It also prevents you getting into the bad habit of tipping the front ball downwards, which you would then have to spend time unlearning later.

Especially revise Exercise 5.1: Holding a Pyramid. Whenever you revise a lesson, try to be a little more strict with your technique than previously. In this case concentrate on improving the flatness of the base to ensure that no gaps open up between the balls of the pyramid.

Lesson 12: Palmspinning 3 Balls in One Hand

Practise lessons 11, 12 and 13 concurrently (preparation for 3 balls in one hand, palmspinning 3 balls in one hand and thumb-lifts and pinky-lifts). Don't expect instant success with 3 balls, but with attention to technique you will make steady progress.

Ex 12.1 Automatic Palmspinning Machine
10 min

Hold 3 acrylics in your hand in a triangle. Place a similarly sized stage ball on top and twist it using your free hand. The stage ball is sticky and will make the 3 balls on the bottom rotate as if they were palmspinning. Then marvel at the wonder that is:

The Automatic Palmspinning Machine™

Pat. Pend. Copyright, Etc

"More Tea Vicar?"

Make sure the 3 balls on the bottom remain horizontal. By practising this and the next exercise your hand will learn to control 3 balls while they are rotating. Start trying to gradually push the balls around with your bottom hand, and soon you will be palmspinning.

Keep it smooth and slow.

At first holding 3 balls in one hand will feel **huge**. Don't worry, with time your hands will become accustomed to them and you'll find them a more manageable handful.

Health Warning

Palmspinning can be very beneficial to your hand-health, but **not** if you push it too hard. Always be careful when you are adding an extra ball.

Palmspinning carries the risk of RSI. Please warm up and take things carefully. If you start to feel discomfort in your fingers or wrists, you are overdoing it. Take a break. See page 6.

Duration: 55 minutes first time. Should be repeated several times.
Balls: 3 acrylics or similar and 1 stage ball of a similar size.

Which Direction?

Inwards or Outwards
At first, there is nothing wrong with focusing on whichever direction you find easiest - until you feel you have achieved an understanding of the technique.

But the sooner you start investing practice time in trying both hands and both directions, the better technique you will develop.

Ex 12.2 Cheat with the Other Hand
15 min

Cheating helps you learn! Try slowly palmspinning while cheating by using the other hand to gently push the triangle of balls around. Your bottom hand should focus on holding the balls in shape so that no gaps appear between them.

Ex 12.3 Go for it: Palmspin 3 in One Hand
15 min

You've done all the preparation, now it's time to start 3 balls in one hand.

Focus on the following details:
Posture: Sit with good posture. Make sure your shoulders are level and relaxed and your that elbow is not touching your body. Smile!

Slow: Palmspinning is not a race, the slower you spin, the quicker you learn.

Horizontal: Make sure you keep the 3 balls flat.

Place a book or CD on top to check the balls are flat. Pictured is the case for the CD "KY" by LemonJelly, a great album for practising Contact. (It is possible to balance a book or CD case on top of the 3 balls whilst palmspinning but this is harder than palmspinning a 4 ball pyramid.)

(Cont...)

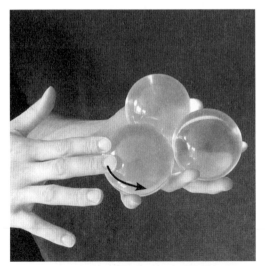

The other hand can also help stop the balls falling off the inside of your palm

Check that your triangle is horizontal

Not horizontal - tipped down at the front

Don't be tempted to let the front of your hand dip downwards! Dipping will make 3 balls a little bit easier at the moment, but it is a bad habit that will take a long time to unlearn later when you want to add a fourth ball to make a pyramid.

Pressure: When you are holding the triangle, keep the pressure even and smooth.

Control: Every click is a mistake, it indicates a momentary loss of control of the balls. Silence is the sign of a master palmspinner. This is a lot more work, and it is much harder - but well worth the effort.

Take it easy. If you start to feel discomfort in your fingers or wrists, you're overdoing it - take a break and practise more of the 2 in one hand exercises.

Good luck.

Ex 12.4 Lesson 4 with 3 balls

15 min

Technique, technique, technique. A lot of the technique you need for great 3 ball palmspinning is in Lesson 4: 2 ball palmspinning.

A great practice session would be to repeat Lesson 4, Exercises 4.4 to 4.9 with 3 balls. Especially the ultra slow and eyes shut exercises. The comments made on page 55 about internal methods of palmspinning and "energy" are very relevant here.

Style Hint

Don't change direction from inward to outward rotations simply by stopping and reversing - it doesn't look smooth. Instead, introduce one pinky-lift to change direction and your inwards and outwards palmspinning will be blended into one smooth transfer. You will meet pinky-lifts in the next chapter...

Ex 13.1 Thumb-lifts - Inward

`15 min`

You will probably find thumb-lifts and pinky-lifts are easier to learn than palmspinning 3 balls, because only 2 balls are moving.

Duration: 1 hour first time. Should be repeated several times.
Balls: 3 acrylics or similar.

1 Start by holding 3 balls in one hand. Wrap your little finger around the back ball to hold the ball into your palm. The back ball doesn't change position in a thumb-lift, only the front 2 balls will change places.

2 Lift the ball. Start the lift not with the tip of your thumb, but by rolling it up from the base of your thumb to the tip. The lifted ball will feel like it is counter-rotating slightly in the direction of the grey arrow. Encourage this rotation so that the ball slides over the other 2 balls.

3 Reach up with your ring finger before the lifted ball gets to the top, so the ball is held by both the thumb and ring finger at the top. Once your thumb has lost contact it is free to hold the back ball. This allows your pinky to help lower the lifted ball. Roll the lifted ball down your ring finger.

4 As you bring the top ball down, transfer the front ball towards your thumb.

Holding the back ball using the pinky, then the thumb, will help to stop the bottom balls separating. Separating would cause them to click back together at the end of the movement, breaking flow.

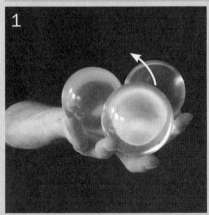
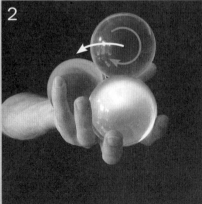
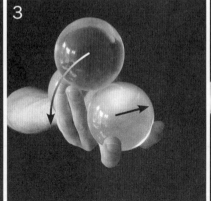
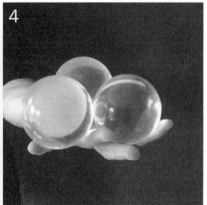

Ex 13.2 Pinky-lifts - Outward

These are the reverse of thumb-lifts. I have no idea why they're called pinky-lifts, it's your ring finger that does most of the lifting.

I dislike the Americanism - "pinky", but I have to use it, sorry. The English name -"little finger" is just too clunky to use here.

1 Start by holding a flat 3 ball triangle with your thumb holding the back ball in place. Begin the motion with the ball nearest to your pinky lifting and rolling up along your ring finger and your pinky.

2 When it has risen halfway, the pinky will no longer be able to support it. Continue lifting it on the ring finger only (it will be held in place by the groove between the other 2 balls). Close your pinky around the back ball.

This will free your thumb to reach up for the ball coming over the top. Your thumb should touch the top ball before it loses contact with your ring finger.

Encourage a slight feeling of counter-rotation in the ball as shown by the black arrow.

3 As the ball gets to the top, use your index and middle fingers to push the front bottom ball towards your pinky, and roll the top ball down your thumb.

4 Finish by lowering down to horizontal, and release the back ball with your pinky, making space for the front ball to roll out onto the pinky.

Return to step 1.

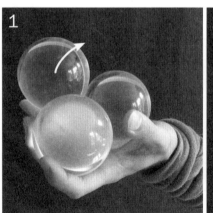
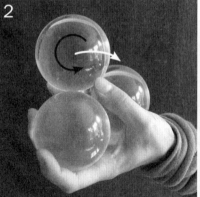

Ex 13.3 Back Exchanges & Shuffling
`15 min`

In the lifts in the last 2 exercises, the front 2 balls changed places, while the back ball stayed in one position - the back of the palm.

That's the easier way to do lifts, but not the only way. You could also hold the front ball in place and exchange the back balls in every lift, making continuous back exchanges either with thumb or pinky-lifts.

I never do these back-lifts continuously, because the front lifts feel better, but they are useful for the incredibly groovy move: shuffling.

Shuffling is simply:
- One front thumb-lift
- One back thumb-lift
- One front thumb-lift
- One back thumb-lift etc

Or alternatively, alternating front and back pinky-lifts. Super good.

Ex 13.4 3 Ball Tango
`15 min`

Try 3 ball palmspinning and lifts moving between many different positions around your body.

Here are some extra ideas to explore and add to 3 ball Tango:
- 3 ball holding and transfers (Lesson 5 with a ball missing)
- Incorporate a 3 ball Snake (Lessons 6 and 9 with a ball missing)
- Separating into 2 in one hand, and 1 ball Tango with the other
- 3 ball Curls both holding and palmspinning (Lesson 7).

Time to go shopping

Because you're ready to try working on three balls in each hand, both hands at the same time, that's 6 balls. But to do that, you may need to buy some more balls.

Take a look at the 6 ball Mind Games and Spaceships (page 107).

3 Balls Many Different Ways

Now you have a whole load of techniques to practise:

- Palmspinning inwards
- Palmspinning outwards
- Thumb-lifts front
- Thumb-lifts back
- Thumb-lift shuffling
- Pinky-lifts front
- Pinky-lifts back
- Pinky-lift shuffling

All of those, and with both left and right hands makes 16 things to practise!

Don't be surprised if it takes a few months to get them all smooth.

If you haven't already, you should look at the inspiration section now. You are ready to try much of the 3 ball chapter and a good few moves from the 4 ball and snakes chapters too.

The 4 ball Funky Pyramid Dodge (page 88) and 4 ball Sticky Ball (page 90) use the 3 ball technique from the last two lessons to great effect.

Remember the controlled rolling in Lessons 2 and 3? Here's where that same technique gets exciting - with 3 balls.

Here, separated palmspinning technique allows the balls to flow smoothly between your hands without any unnecessary clicks or clunks.

Duration: 1 hour 10 minutes first time. Should be repeated several times.
Balls: 3 balls. Acrylics, stage balls, silicones or oranges are all fine. It will help a little with the 423 exercises if you have one ball a different colour to the others, if not, use your imagination.

Preparation

To warm up for this lesson, revise Lesson 2, especially Exercise 2.4 which is like this lesson but with only 1 ball. Being comfortable with the palm roll walks in Lesson 3 will also help.

Posture

These moves force your elbows inwards in a 'cleavage-enhancing' pose. If you practise these with your hands down at waist level, you will end up hunching your shoulders, your head will go down, you will restrict your breathing and you will give yourself backache.

Instead, present these moves by lifting them up to chest height. Try not to hold your arms fixed in one position - your arms will tire less if you gently move them around.

Ex 14.1 Cascade
10 min

Three ball cascade. Keep it slow and smooth with controlled rolling, not gravity rolling.

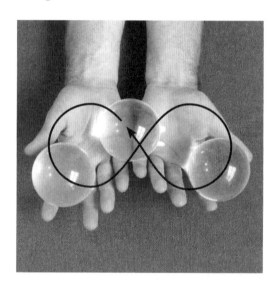

Keep the speed of the balls constant around the whole path. Avoid the temptation to "chuck" them quickly across the back of the palm just because you feel you don't have control there.

Try also the reverse direction, with the balls coming forward across the palms.

Ex 14.2 Loop
`10 min`

If you find that the tricky bit of this move is the straight roll across the back of the palms, practise this again with 1 ball, and then 2 balls. Try to focus on keeping the speed of the balls constant and controlled, and as before, resist the temptation to "chuck" the ball across quickly at the back.

Try both directions, anti-clockwise and clockwise.

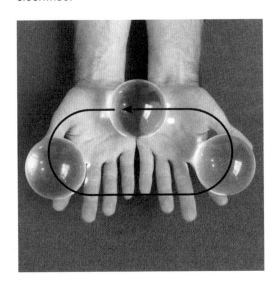

Ex 14.3 2 in One Hand Transitions
`10 min`

Practise changing between the Cascade, and 2 in one hand in either hand. Then practise the same transition with Loops and finally practise using a little bit of 2 in one hand to change between loops and cascades.

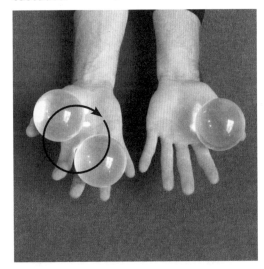

Initially just hold the third ball stationary, and make the 2 palmspinning balls the focus. Then experiment with the third ball, make it the focus. Move it around with 1 ball Tango or make it visually interact with the 2 palmspinning balls (see 3 ball Sticky Ball page 84).

Ex 14.4 423
`10 min`

Four-Two-Three is a particular combination of a cascade and 2 in one hand.

Start with 2 balls in your right hand (one clear and one black) and 1 clear ball in your left hand. Throughout the move focus your attention on the black ball.

1 Separated-palmspin inwards the 2 balls in your right hand until the black comes to the middle, then...

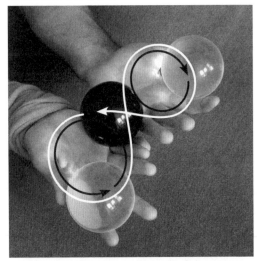

The black ball is always swapping hands doing a cascade pattern (white arrow) while the 2 clear balls never change hands (black arrows).

2 Cascade-pass the black ball into your left hand. This brings you to the mirror image of the start position. Now repeat on the other side.

3 Separated-palmspin three-quarters of a rotation inwards with the 2 balls in your left hand.

4 Watch the black ball. When it comes back into the middle, you're ready to Cascade-pass the black ball back into the right hand.

In this basic 423 style, the black ball is always the one that changes hands, and all the palmspinning is inwards.

When you think you've got it, confuse yourself by trying the reverse - 423 with all the palmspinning rolling outwards.

423 is the name for a basic 3 ball juggling pattern in a geeky juggling notation called "siteswap". This is the same pattern made using 3 balls palmspinning, hence the name.

1 Separated-palmspin 2 balls inwards. Then cross your hands with 1 ball in the lower hand.

2 Transfer down 1 ball from the top hand. The ball should leave the palm between thumb and index finger. Switch which hand is on top, then repeat on the other side.

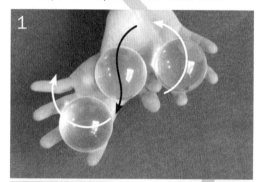

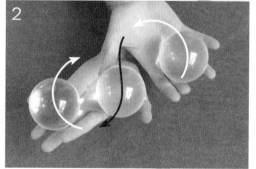

This is one of the best looking tricks in separated palmspinning - 423 with the black ball completely isolated throughout the movement.

The isolated black ball is the one that changes hands. The 2 other balls stay in their respective hands and make elliptical orbits.

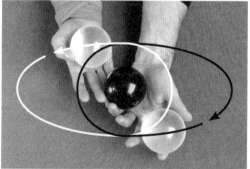

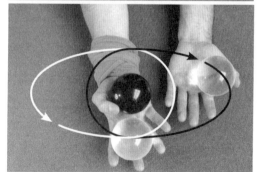

As shown, each hand will make only half a rotation of isolated separated palmspinning before passing the black ball back to the other hand.

This is a difficult move, but well worth the effort - good luck!

A great variation of this is to combine it with the Crossed Transfer to get the 423 Isolated Crossed Transfer! Each hand will now need to palmspin one full rotation before passing the black ball.

Ex 14.7 423 Loops
10 min

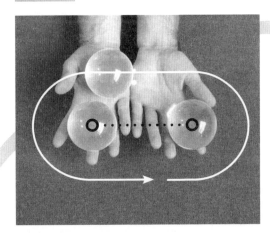

What do you get if you make your 423 with one hand palmspinning inwards and the other palmspinning outwards? "423 Loops", of course.

Super style tip
Hold 2 of the balls in position and make it appear that they are connected by an imaginary rod. These 2 fixed balls will be isolated when each is part of the palmspin and simply held in position when alone in the hand (later, as an advanced version, isolate the held ball).

The effect you get is 2 balls fixed in space while the third runs in a track around them.

Adv Ex 14.8 423 with 2 Balls Isolated

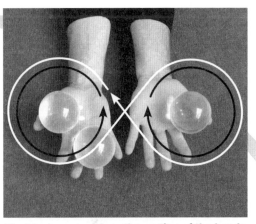

The black arrows show the motion of the hands isolating the 2 stationary balls. The white arrow is the figure-8 path of the middle ball.

This 3 ball Mind Game is the sister to the previous exercise. This is 423 with the 2 balls permanently fixed in space, again connected by an imaginary rod.

The vanilla (easier) version is simply to hold the solo ball in your hand while it is not palmspinning (as with 423 loops). The advanced variation is to use palm circle isolations which you will meet in Lesson 16. Learn the vanilla/held version now, and return to the palm circle isolation variation later.

3 Ball Mind Games

When you feel you have made some progress with the isolations in Lesson 16, return to this lesson and try exploring 3 ball Mind Games with variations of 423 with 1 ball isolated and with 2 balls isolated.

There are many variations which combine together into beautiful and mesmerising sequences of 3 ball Mind Games. This is a richly rewarding area of Multiball Contact to explore.

Here are some ideas to play with:

○ Cascade with 1 ball isolated! Or even better (and easier), mix isolated cascade with a bit of 2 in one hand, in geeky siteswap that would be 42333 or 4242333. If you don't understand siteswap, don't worry. I recommend you never learn it!

○ Add 2 in one hand and Tango with the solo ball. It can connect and visually interact with the 2 palmspinning balls.

○ A beautiful variation of the 423 loop is to isolate the loop ball, whilst keeping the other 2 balls still connected by the imaginary rod. The balls should keep the same separation and the rod should still stay aligned on the east-west axis, so that as one unit they will orbit the other ball.

○ Play with variations in speed.

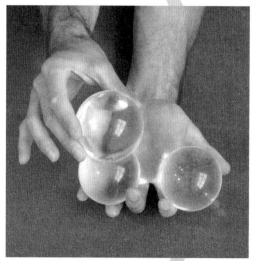

Tango with the solo ball, make it connect with the palmspinning balls

○ A magical moment in 3 ball Mind Games is the transition of a ball into and out of isolation - explore that. For example changing from 423 to 423 with 1 or 2 balls isolated.

○ Move the balls around: good Mind Games have isolations and dynamic movement, and variations of positions. Playing in one position is all too easy a trap to fall into. While 3 in two hands is quite constraining, there is still some room for movement. Take the balls out to the side, stand up, carry them above your head, or down to the ground. Isolations will help as they force you to move your hands around.

○ Add into the mix 3 in one hand, and any of the moves from the 3 ball inspiration section.

Lesson 15: Palmspinning a Pyramid

In Pyramids, the top ball has an irritating tendency to fall off. And it adds extra pressure, trying to force the 3 balls of the base apart.

Here is a lesson that will help you with the step up from 3 to 4 balls. There's nothing new that you'll need to learn, but it's going to take a lot of effort and time spent polishing your technique to get your pyramids easy

Duration: Months.
Balls: 4 Acrylics or similar.

Ready for 4 balls?

and relaxed.

First, review your 3 ball technique with a critical eye. All the effort you put into clean palmspinning technique will pay off here.

When your 3 in one hand feels relaxed and smooth, and is consistently flat (it doesn't have to be completely click free...yet), you will be ready to progress to practising palmspinning with a 4 ball pyramid.

Small clicks usually don't need to be ironed out completely for a pyramid to work - you can eliminate those later. But the flatter and quieter you have your 3 balls, the easier it will be to step up to 4 balls.

If you get separations and loud "clicks" in your 3 balls, it's time to put in a few hours polishing before you move on to the next stage.

Posture & Speed

Warm up and sit well. Palmspinning is not meant to be a race. Slow, smooth, relaxed and in control. And remember to enjoy it!

Ex 15.1 Stage Ball

15 min

This is a great intermediate step - put a stage ball on top of your 3 ball triangle, and palmspin it as shown below. A stage ball is lighter than an acrylic, so it puts less pressure on the bottom balls (therefore causing less separating).

If the stage ball repeatedly falls off the top, you're probably not holding your base flat. Repeat the CD case exercise (page 61), and work again on making your 3 balls completely flat.

Palmspin with a stage ball on top

71

Ex 15.2 Cheat with Your Other Hand
15 min

Once you can get the pyramid spinning with a stage ball on top, it's time to try 4 acrylics. At first use your free hand (as shown below) when necessary to help hold the base in shape and to stop balls escaping from the inside of your hand. With time you will develop the extra finger strength needed for the extra weight.

Great training is to make Pyramid Tango (Lesson 5), but start to add a small amount of palmspinning. Try one shift (a third of a rotation) in each hold position.

Ex 15.3 Thumb-lifts & Pinky-lifts with a Pyramid
15 min

Revise the 3 ball lifts lesson, with an extra ball! Concentrate on not letting the top 2 balls separate as they go up and over the top. If you have smaller hands or larger balls there is a chance that thumb-lifts and pinky-lifts may not be possible, or may be very difficult.

A good exercise to help with lifts is to practise holding a pyramid in the intermediate position shown below. Gently rock it back and forth without letting the top balls separate.

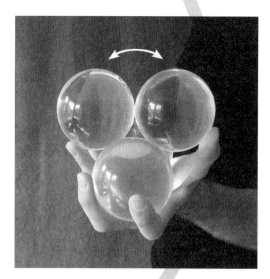

After a Pyramid

Once upon a time, 4 balls in each hand was the pinnacle of palmspinning... But now, even with large balls (85mm diameter) five in one hand is possible in a square-based pyramid - see the 5 ball Inspiration Section (page 105).

If you want to pursue the path of smaller balls, you'll find it possible to palmspin 6, 7, or even more balls in each hand. See the Small Balls Inspiration Section (page 133).

For now, if you can spin a pyramid - even if it is done badly, congratuations. If you can spin a pyramid smoothly, then you are an accomplished palmspinner. If you can spin a pyramid smoothly, with no clicks, in both hands, in both directions and in many different positions around your body, then you can feel justifiably proud that you have mastered this technique.

Lesson 16: Palm Circle Isolations

This is **the** isolation in Ball Contact - a fundamental move. The concept is simple: with one ball on your palm, move your hand in circles while keeping the ball stationary in space - hence "isolation". This is the killer move of illusion-based Contact - the effect of the ball magically floating is mesmerising.

This isolation is one of the hardest moves in Contact, because the more you practise polishing it, the more you notice its imperfections.

Learning to "isolate" badly is very easy. To gain very clean and slow isolations you'll have to train a lot with this perfect meditation exercise.

Duration: 45 minutes first time.
Ball: A 75 to 100mm (3" to 4") acrylic ball is ideal. Use the largest acrylic you have, as larger, heavier balls are more stable and so are easier to get clean isolations with. However, to keep from injuring your fingers avoid using anything that is too heavy for you.
Stage balls are harder to isolate cleanly because their low mass makes them easy to accidentally bump out of the isolation.

Warm Up Exercises:

After stretching your fingers, wrists and arms, it will help to warm up by revising the following:

- 1 ball palm rolling exercises (Lessons 2 and 3)
- Some gentle 2 ball palmspinning
- 2 ball separated palmspinning isolations (Lesson 10)

Ex 16.1 Cat Claw
15 min

Practise your isolations by cheating and holding the ball in place with the fingernails of your other hand sliding on the acrylic. Move the bottom hand in even, controlled circles under the ball.

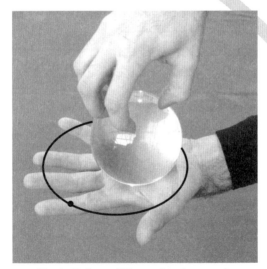

The ball stays still, your hand moves in circles under the ball

Technique tips are on the following page. At first your top hand (the "cat claw") will be doing lots of work to keep the ball in place. Your focus should be on smoothing out the bottom hand, so that the cat claw is barely doing any of the work to hold the ball in isolation and is only very lightly touching the ball.

Isolation Superhints

These Superhints apply to all the isolation exercises in this lesson. If you can start applying them from the start, you won't have to unlearn bad habits later.

Which direction?

To start with, most people find it easier to roll inwards so the ball travels out from the palm over the thumb. Ultimately practise both hands and both directions.

Posture

Sit or stand well. Relax. Ensure your shoulders are level and lift the ball up. Isolations look good at chest height, which is where most performers present them. I made the mistake of learning all my isolations at waist height, and had to retrain later.

Present the ball

Don't let your fingers close up - it looks bad. Try to spread your hand and fingers open all the time so that you're offering the ball. This is much harder to do but will make your isolation look and feel 10 times better.

Isolations are not a race

There is nothing to be gained from rushing to move a ball nowhere! Great isolations can be as slow as one orbit every 2-3 seconds. Try to slow down all the fast bits so that the roll has a smooth and even speed, and never goes quick-slow-quick-slow.

Look and align

In order to help fix your isolations in space you will need to look at them closely and check that the ball is not moving (technically it would be correct to say "not translating", see box on page 16). Either look at the edge of the ball and keep it aligned with an object in the background or alternatively, if it is a clear acrylic ball, look at the image in the ball, and hold that steady.

Use a mirror

Practise with a mirror placed in many different positions to your side and in front of you. This will allow you to check that the ball is stationary from many different views and angles. You can then make sure that the ball is isolated in all planes: up/down, side to side and front/back.

Ex 16.2 Ultra Slow Ninja Palm Circle Isolations
15 min

An exercise in three parts: the palm, the fingers and finally the complete palm circle, all the time practising going really, really, REALLY, slowly.

One orbit of your hand every 1 to 2 minutes: almost stationary.

The palm
To do this, divide the path across the back of your palm - between your pinky and your thumb - into 8 to 12 stop positions, and move between these positions. Hold the ball in each position in complete control, then move to the next position. Practise just the palm half-circle for a few minutes.

The fingers
Feel another 8 to 12 positions for the ball between the tip of your thumb and pinky across the fingers - the other half of the circle. You should find stopping on the fingers a lot easier than on the palm. Practise the finger half-circle for a few minutes.

Palm circle
Full circle, isolating, as slooooow as you can. Do it with a constant lack of speed all around the circle, pausing and taking a breath in every position.

This exercise will revolutionise your palm isolations. Do this for 10 minutes, or as long as you can take it. First time, most people can only take a few minutes before they go a bit loopy.

Repeat this exercise several times over the weeks or months you are learning isolations. Each time you return to a more normal speed, you will feel the improvement.

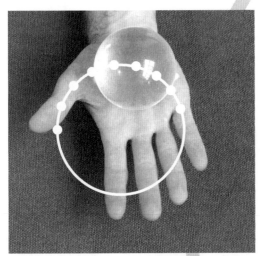

Ultra slow rolling across the back of the palm between stop positions

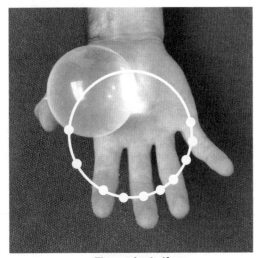

The easier half

Ex 16.3 Palm Circle
15 min Isolations

Go for it! A lot of practice time is needed to get rock solid isolations with both hands in both directions. All the technique hints are in the Isolations Superhints box on the previous spread.

Once you've got the basic isolation movement sussed, you can move it around, to add to the effect.

Isolations - they're not like riding a bike! If you don't practise, your isolations can become rusty4, and it takes a long time to re-learn them. So once you got 'em, don't let 'em go.

Congratulations

That's it, the end of the last lesson. If you've completed all 16 lessons of Multiball Contact, then well done!

Some of these moves, especially from the later lessons, are going to take weeks or even months to polish, with numerous repetitions of each lesson. Have a second look at all the advanced exercises at the end of each lesson; there's a lot to explore there.

Time to start exploring the full potential of what you can do with these techniques next... in the Inspiration Section.

The following often repeated statements are not totally correct:

"There's no substitute for the 3 P's: practice, practice and practice".

"There are no easy moves in Contact".

It's true that Contact will take you a lot of practice to master, perhaps even years of work, but the key is not just **how much** you practise, it is **how** you practise.

Here's a concept: Not all practice is good for your technique. It's quite possible to practise bad technique which you will later have to spend time unlearning and correcting with good technique!

The following pages suggest training methods which you may find useful when exploring Contact and when learning new moves in the Inspiration Section.

Play!

While this book might continuously harp on about technique and training, it's not fun just to focus on these all the time.

Enjoy your practice sessions. Contact is meant to be fun. Human brains learn better when they are enjoying themselves. You will gain much from switching off your conscious critical mind and just playing.

Try not to get annoyed with your mistakes - take time to enjoy every drop you make!

Training

When you are training (as opposed to playing), work out what is good technique for a particular move, then focus on refining that technique.

Mentally visualise yourself doing a move that you want to learn, and try practising with an imaginary ball (you may wish to do this in private!).

Try structuring your training sessions and keeping a record of your progress. You'll probably find that you are learning much more than you realise.

As well as working towards doing moves that you **can't** do, experiment with trying to stretch outwards in little steps from moves that you **can** do.

Take a few lessons in Tai Chi, dance or other systems of movement. Choose whichever appeals to you. Find good teachers, who teach in a style that you get on with.

Find a good teacher for Contact; again one who teaches in a way that you can learn from.

Warm Up & Cool Down

Physically and mentally warm up and cool down before you pick up the ball (see page 6).

As with any sport or skill, contact juggling is very psychological. You will probably find that contact juggling affects your mental state, and conversely, your mental state affects your contact juggling - hopefully in a good way, of course.

Revise

After you think that you've learned and read everything in a lesson or a chapter, try reading it one more time, you may find that you gain new nuggets of technique.

If you don't learn directly from re-reading the words on the page, they may blend with the thoughts in your head, and help generate new ideas for your play.

Watch & Copy

Learning is about copying initially; this is why children and babies have an innate tendency to copy, it's a natural step in the learning process.

Watch lots of Contact, manipulation, martial arts and dance. If you can't watch it in real life, watch videos. See www. MinistryofManipulation.com for links to Contact and manipulation videos.

Trying to re-invent all these moves might be fun, but it would waste a heck of a long time, - especially when you already have a copy of this book! Learn the techniques in the lessons, but don't stop there, watch and copy, then adapt.

The real joy is to take each move further, to give each of those moves your own style, to make them your own, and to develop new moves with new techniques.

Polish

It's very tempting to move on and learn another trick, rather than polishing what you've already got. Try to resist this temptation, if you want to be a great manipulator, you've got to polish what you've got.

If your audience is made of folk who play with balls, they may be impressed by you *just managing* to do really hard tricks with poor presentation.

But if your audience is made of civilians (those who are not obsessed with balls) then they are most likely to be wowed by great presentation of moves that you have solid.

What to you seems to be simple material, non-contact jugglers will find very fascinating, especially if it is presented cleanly, with care and attention to the way you do the trick.

It doesn't have to be difficult to be beautiful.

Train With a Mirror

Use a mirror, and try to watch yourself, not the ball. If you have access to one, use a video camera.

Play Slower

The slower you practise the quicker you will learn. It may help to link all of your Contact movements to your breathing – a technique which is fundamental to Yoga and many martial arts.

Sequences
ABC BAC & ABCBAC

Practise sequences, not individual tricks. Pick 3 moves that you are starting to get solid, let's call them "A", "B" and "C".

Now link them together in the sequence ABC. Practise this with a short flowing movement to connect A to B to C. The exciting bits here are the transitions, not the tricks. Try to make the elements of the sequence as short as possible, for example if your "B" is a palmspin then your could do only one palmspin, or even half a palmspin. Learn to do this sequence in both hands - and polish it.

Next, make the similar sequence BAC. And finally put the two together, and run them continuously ABC-BAC-ABC-BAC....
Learn and polish this longer sequence until it is fluid in both hands.

Look for the moments of magic in these sequences and keep those parts - later they will help you make routines.

This exercise helps you learn how to make transitions from one trick to any other trick. It also helps you break out of a rut and establish new patterns and sequences.

Learn a Routine

Learn a routine, your own routine and not somebody else's!

Make yourself a learning routine. The purpose of this routine is to help you polish and practise material, not to devise or choreograph a show.

Choose a piece of music and fill it with sequences - mini routines like the one suggested previously. You may find it helps when making each mini routine to pick a start and finish position, then fill in the gap with 10-30 seconds of tricks.

When you are constructing a learning routine, try not to be too critical about which moves go in it in which order. This is for practice, not for performance. If you want to be critical, critique your technique and presentation. Polish these routines like crazy.

Then later, if you choose to make a show routine, you may take some parts of your best learning sequences, and include them as building blocks in your show routine.

Should you Learn a Move in Both Hands at Once?

Yes...
... and No.

For each trick, you will have a strong hand and a weak hand. The main difference is that one hand has had a lot more practice manipulating than the other.

If you are learning from a good teacher who is helping you with technique, then it's good to learn both hands at once.

If you are learning on your own, there is going to be a bit of stumbling around in the dark - technique wise. So it's usually a good idea to favour one hand while you are working out the correct technique, without ignoring your weak hand completely. Each hand will make a different mistake, and therefore teach you different details about the move.

Then, as soon as you're happy with the technique in your strong hand, you'll find it easy to transfer to the weak hand.

In everyday life, one hand, usually the right hand, gets to do all of the writing, and most of the picking up, brushing of teeth, and other daily tasks, so it has better control.

As you practise Contact, your non-writing hand will gain more control and co-ordination. Writing is not the pinnacle of human dexterity, You could learn to be ambidextrous, to write or to brush your teeth with your wrong hand if you practised. Come to think of it, brushing your teeth with the wrong hand is a great exercise to help with improving your co-ordination.

Musicality

Be aware of the connection of your movement with the music.

Match the mood and style of your Contact with the music you are performing or playing to.

Musicality is something I've been teaching at juggling convention workshops for several years. If you want to know more about it, come to one of my workshops, or visit www.MinistryofManipulation.com for details.

Online Forums

Visit online forums for Contact, Juggling and Manipulation such as www.ContactJuggling.org, for great advice, chat and video clips.

Multiball
Inspiration
Section

Presentation

You don't need to learn a lot of Contact material to look good doing Contact, you need good presentation.

One of my favourite contact juggling performers makes 90% of his routine out of only three tricks, but he does those three tricks VERY well and involves a lot of variation and body movement and always draws the crowd, even when he is practising. He has a lot more material, but as a professional he knows what works and how to present it.

Don't hide behind the ball. You are presenting **your** Contact; you and the ball. Here are some points to consider as part of your presentation:

Style
The lessons in this book teach a pure style of Contact, with emphasis on smoothness, and slow controlled rolling, on clean lines and posture.

There are few frills or flourishes in this pure style. I consider it to be the "basic" style I use for teaching, but it is not the only way to do things and beautiful effects can often be created by doing the opposite.

Style and presentation are as important as technique. Experiment and play with style, develop your own style and add style to each basic technique and move.

Posture
Stand up or sit up straight and keep your shoulders open, not hunched. If you have a ball in one hand, be careful not to let that shoulder drop.

Free arm
Playing Contact with one hand hanging limply by your side while the other arm is holding the balls is usually a clear sign that a manipulator is not aware of their presentation. It is called a "dead fish arm".

Bring your other arm into the action, here's some ideas to start you off:
- Get your free arm involved in the action, moving around and interacting with the ball and your other arm.
- Keep your free arm alive. It can be by your side, but in a slightly alive or ready posture rather than hanging limply.
- Mirror the other hand, but without the ball.
- Sometimes it works to tuck it out of the way and hide it behind your back.

Face and head
"Avoid Making Silly Faces" - Rich Shumaker. It's best to avoid the "I'm concentrating so hard that I've stuck my tongue out" facial expression. Choose your facial expression with care and let your face show emotion - Smile!

Eyes
Don't stare at the ball.* Try moving your focus from being internal – "me and the ball" to include the world and people who may be watching you. Your eyes are a powerful tool for connecting with other people.

In order to practise this, make an imaginary audience in your training space using toy robots, potted plants, teddy bears and pictures on the wall. Make eye contact with each of these audience members while you train.

* Although staring into the ball can be effective, if when performing you wish to create a "gazing into a magic ball" feeling. But try not to fall into the habit of making it your default presentation for Contact.

Three balls is a versatile number for Contact. This chapter gives some ideas to get you started.

3 ball contact in the lessons section:
- Holding a Triangle - Lessons 5 (with only 3 balls).
- Palmspinning - Lessons 11, 12 & 13.
- 3 Ball Curls - Lesson 7.
- 3 balls in two hands separated - Lesson 14.
- There is also a lot more 3 ball Contact to be explored based upon 1 and 2 ball Contact techniques with an extra ball, and by combining 1 and 2 ball Contact with Toss Juggling (not covered in *Multiball Contact*).

If you have completed Lesson 4 and can palmspin 2 balls in both hands, both directions, you are ready to try most of the material in this section. Your 2 ball palmspinning doesn't have to be that proficient yet, as learning these 3 ball tricks will help you gain control.

1 potato, 2 potato, 3 potato, 4...

1 A very simple trick that feels lovely to do. Start by holding 3 balls in a column.

2 Lift off the top ball with the top hand with an ice cream hold as shown. This leaves the middle ball, in an ice cream hold on the bottom hand.

3 Open your right hand to bring the ball into your palm. Then close your fist around the ball, and push it underneath the left hand in the mirror image of the starting position.

4 Repeat on each side. This can be done in either direction; upwards - as shown, or downwards - the reverse.

3 Ball Sticky Ball

For a simple visual effect, palmspin 2 balls in one hand and in your free hand hold another ball. Keep this single ball continuously stuck to the side of one of the 2 palmspinning balls, so that all 3 balls form a straight line.

This move is exactly the same concept as the sticky ball trick in the 4 ball and 5 ball chapters.

A variation is to try swapping hands while keeping the line and its rotation. That is, passing 1 ball across to alternate which hand is doing the palmspinning.

3 Ball Line

Everything in Lesson 6: Dead Snakes can be done with 3 balls instead of 4. Unsurprisingly, it's much easier with 3 balls. Think of it not as 3 individual balls, but as one object; a line made of 3 balls. You work to maintain the straight line, manipulating it as one object, rather than manipulating 3 individual balls.

Triangle

Hold 3 balls in two hands (below), rotate this triangle over and over by vertical palmspinning as shown by the arrow.

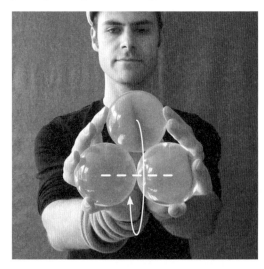

For added style, you could also try isolating this move - either isolate around the bottom 2 balls as shown and rotate the other ball around it, or hold the top ball isolated and run the other 2 balls around.

Most of the 4 ball pyramid holding and manipulating tricks from Lesson 5: Holding a Pyramid can be performed with 3 balls in a triangle.

3 Ball Pouring

From 3 ball palmspinning inwards, you can pour all 3 balls in succession into the other hand. Bring the empty hand up from underneath and pour the balls through the gap between the thumb and the index finger as shown. When they arrive in the second hand they should also be palmspinning inwards. There will inevitably be some clicking as the balls close back together to form a triangle.

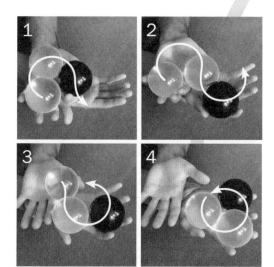

3 Ball Ratchet

1 In your right hand palmspin 2 balls outward with one of them isolated. In your left hand hold a third ball stationary beside the isolated ball.

2,3,4 The orbiting ball of the palmspin can only make three quarters of a revolution before it meets the held ball. Release the held ball into your right palm...

5 ... and start palmspinning all 3 balls. A fraction of a rotation later, the black ball which was previously orbiting will arrive in your left hand.

6 Hold it there for three quarters of a revolution until the orbiting clear ball comes to swap with it again. And you're back to step 1.

In every rotation, the orbiting ball and the held ball swap places.

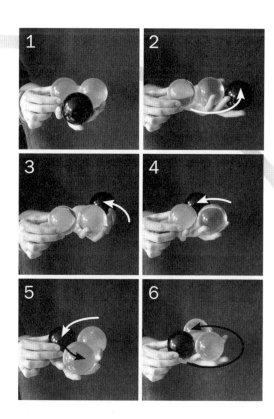

3 Balls in One Hand Cascade

This is palmspinning with the balls travelling in a figure 8 pattern in one hand. It doesn't feel smooth to do as the balls clunk together each time they come back to the middle of your hand, but it can look great. Follow steps 1-6 below. Step 7 would be the same as step 1 with each ball moved one position clockwise round the palm.

You can think of it as a series of 2 ball palmspinning exchanges while holding a third ball in the hand. First, anti-clockwise with the front 2 balls (1-3), then clockwise with the back 2 balls (4-6).

Or it can be thought of as alternately shuffling balls through the middle - a ball from the back (black ball in figure 2) then a ball from the front (white ball in figure 5).

Palmspinning Isolations

Two ball Isolated palmspinning was the first exercise in Lesson 8: Mind Games. Now add another ball.

With 3 balls, as well as flat palmspinning, you can thumb-lift and pinky-lift the isolated ball – while keeping it isolated, for an awesome effect.

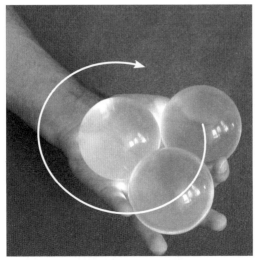

Isolated palmspinning

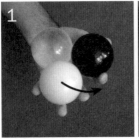
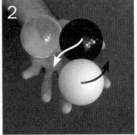
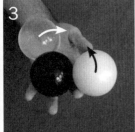
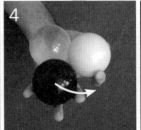
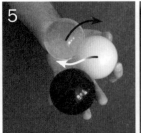
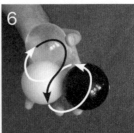

Palmspinning Separated:
3 balls in One Hand

B eing able to smoothly spin three 3" acrylics separated in one hand is fiendishly difficult - **much** harder than a 4 ball pyramid (touching) and probably as hard as palmspinning 5 of those same balls in a pyramid (touching).

If you want to learn it, I recommend you get your 4 ball pyramids super smooth first.

Here is a great learning tip:
Spinning a pyramid of 4 sticky balls (or 3 acrylics and 1 sticky ball) separated is easier than spinning just 3 of those balls

separated. I know it sounds crazy but what happens is that the top sticky ball helps to hold the 3 base balls apart. Practise spinning a base with 3 acrylics and a sticky stage ball on top:

Learn with a stage ball on top first, then 3 in one hand separated is easier!

To learn 3 separated, go back through all the exercises in Lessons 4 and 12 for palmspinning 2 and 3 balls, repeating them with this arrangement of 3 acrylic balls separated with 1 stage ball on the top.

For example, repeat Lesson 4: Exercise 4.2, this time practise holding this separated pyramid with a point in each of the positions North, South, East and West.

Another great learning tip: Try 3 balls in one hand separated with smaller balls, and gradually work up to large balls.

More 3 balls

1 & 2 ball Contact with an extra ball
There is a huge range of moves created by taking 1 and 2 ball Contact techniques of rolling and balancing and adding an extra ball.

3 ball juggling with Contact
Once you start to combine rolling and balancing with throwing, you then have so many possibilities that an entire book could be written on the subject alone.

Four balls rock! There is a **lot** of material with 4 balls - probably as much as there is for 5, 6, 7, 8, 9, 10 and 11 balls combined.

As a general rule, the more balls used in contact juggling, the less versatile it becomes. This chapter looks short but that's because there are a whopping six lessons and three inspiration sections in this book about 4 ball contact. Here is the list:

- Palmspinning: Lessons 10 and 15
- Pyramids: Lessons 5 and 13
- Mind games: Lesson 8
- Snakes: Lesson 9 and the next chapter
- Dead Snakes: Lesson 6
- 3D Snakes: next chapter
- Helical Snakes Workshop after the next chapter

And here are a few more inspiring ideas with 4 balls...

Funky Pyramid Dodge

From a pyramid in your left hand, take the top ball in your right hand, move it slightly forward and do a pinky-lift with the remaining 3 in your left hand. As you do the pinky-lift, keep the black ball in contact with the 2 back balls in the left hand.

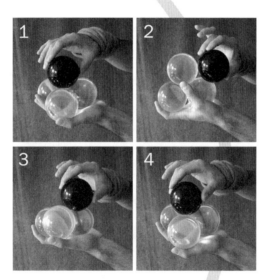

As you finish the pinky-lift, and the 3 balls in the left hand return to flat, replace the black ball on top of the stack. Then repeat the movement, carrying the top ball around the **front** of the stack.

Pyramid Collapse & Reform

Voted "Most cheesy move in multiball" for 8 years running ...

From a pyramid do half a pinky-lift to get to the starting position (1). Then separate the top 2 balls to form a diamond (2).

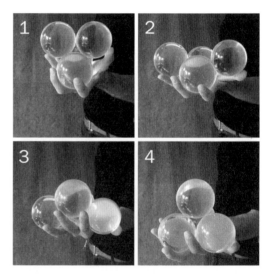

(3) Continue the separation motion and lift the front ball with your fingers. Keep the front and back balls in contact with each other throughout the motion.
(4) Finish the motion by returning back to a pyramid.

"Contact juggling is... looking at my acrylic, calling it a crystal ball and reading my future, which says, "he will have no job and travel and busk for money." - Arnar "

Multiball Contact
4 Ball Inspiration

There is an alternative style for the pyramid collapse and reform move:

(1) Same.
(2) Separate the 2 top balls, stop when all 4 balls become horizontal in your hand in a diamond shape.
(3) Squeeze in the 2 side balls until they touch, to form a diamond pointing the other way.
(4) Push the front ball of the diamond up with you fingers to reform the pyramid (4).

For extra cheese, use your free hand to mime these motions without touching the balls:
(1) Mime lifting one side of the pyramid to cause the pinky-lift to occur.
(2) Mime a chop – to separate the balls.
(3) Mime a squeeze from the sides – to shift the diamond.
(4) Mime the pull up of the front to rebuild the pyramid.

Revolving Door

Relatively easy with 4 high friction balls like stage balls - much harder with slippery balls like acrylics. The technique is simply 2 ball palmspinning. Try to have the pressure smooth and even, and as light as possible without the balls falling out. If you squeeze too hard, this formation will tend to explode, firing a messy pulp of balls all over the room.

You can do it vertically as shown, or horizontally; in either direction, with or without isolation.

Surprisingly, with stage balls, this trick can be done with only one hand, with the other hand being replaced by a flat surface - the floor, a wall, your tummy, or - and here is something funky - a mirror!

Separated Palmspinning: 4 Balls in Two Hands

There is some great material with 4 balls separated, passing between two hands in loops, cascades and more complex patterns, 4 ball separated Tango.

Look at Lesson 14: 3 Balls in Two Hands Separated and Lesson 8: Mind Games, for inspiration. Explore and create.

Revolving Door

4 Ball Sticky Ball

For a simple visual effect, palmspin 3 balls in one hand, including thumb-lifts and pinky-lifts. While in your free

hand holding a fourth ball, which you keep continuously stuck to one of the 3 palmspinning balls. Play with the feeling that the free ball is pulling the triangle around, or the triangle is driving the free ball around. See the 5 ball inspiration section for the 5 ball version: Pyramid and a sticky ball (page 103).

Pyramid Palmspinning Isolations

See 3 ball palmspinning isolations (page 86), and add a fourth ball. The difficulty here comes from holding one ball isolated solidly while 3 balls move around it.

Visually this gets very interesting when you add in isolated thumb-lifts and pinky-lifts, which cause you to have to change the height of your hands.

You will need to put in a lot of time polishing the quality of your isolations before the effect becomes magical.

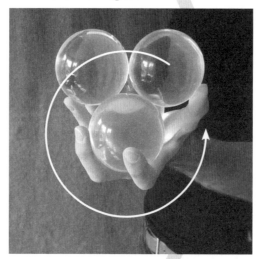

Isolated thumb-lifts - the centre ball is isolated

Palmspinning Flat 4 in One Hand

See 5 in one hand (pages 105-106). You should learn palmspinning 5 in one hand before learning 4 balls in a flat square! The fifth ball helps to make the stack more stable.

Even more 4 balls...

We're not finished with 4 balls yet. The next chapter is about snakes, some of the coolest 4 ball moves.

Snakes

Contact snakes make 4 balls come to life with character and personality, as an animated snake, a wriggling worm and a crawling caterpillar.

The original concepts of contact snakes and trains are accredited to Michael Moschen.

There are two lessons which will help you prepare for this section:

- Lesson 6 - Dead Snakes
- Lesson 9 - The classic Snake motion

The next chapter is also about Snakes - the Advanced Helical Snakes workshop.

Worms

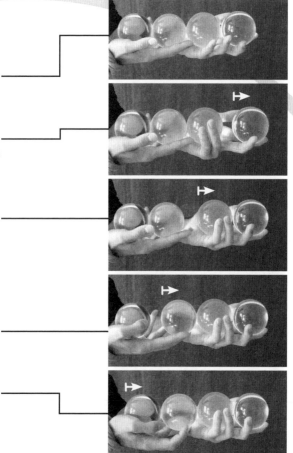

Worms are the baby sister of Snakes. Easy to do, but practice is essential to be able to present them well enough to create the illusion.

1 Make a clean dead snake (4 ball line), holding 2 balls in each hand.

2 Move the front ball forward 20mm by spreading your fingers, while holding the other 3 balls perfectly stationary.

3 Next, move the second ball forward to touch the first. Here you should keep balls 1,3 and 4 stationary (holding the first ball isolated is the difficult part of this movement).

4 Next, move the third ball ...

5 ... then finally the fourth ball.

Repeat, to make your worm crawl slowly along.

Train

Trains are like snakes that go somewhere. Normal "contact snakes" move like a snake, but "trains" move like a train - each ball following the same path along the "rails".

Mentally construct a rail in space, and move the snake along that rail with each ball following the rail - like the carriages of a train.

A good place to start is by imagining a flat figure of 8 in front of you, or to make contours around parts of your body (like your knees while sitting cross-legged) without the balls touching them, or around the edges of furniture or patterns on the floor (again, without touching them).

As you go around a corner, it may help to focus on one point of that corner and make sure that each ball passes through that point.

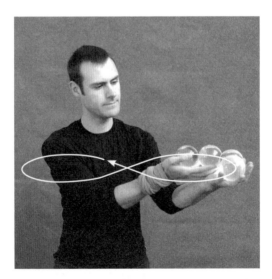

Hanging Rope Snake

Make a 4 ball vertical snake with the top ball isolated to create a funky effect like a swinging rope (see pictures below).

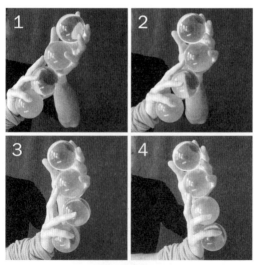

Hanging rope

Digital Snake

Snakes are usually a flowing liquid movement. But what if you are playing Contact to some hard electronic music?

Then your snakes can go digital too. For inspiration watch the movie "Tron" or the computer game "Snake" (with the snake that grows longer everytime it eats a piece of fruit).

Make an imaginary grid, and a path on that grid.

Holding 2 balls in each hand, move the snake one position along the grid path. Make sure all the balls move at the same time, so that they stay in contact. Move once every 4 or 8 beats, so your snake keeps an even rhythm.

Now here's where it starts getting complex - extend your flat two-dimensional grid vertically so that you form a cubic grid in three-dimensional space. Now get busy with a 3D Digital Snake!

Waves

Snakes normally wiggle side-to-side. They can also ripple up-down, like small waves or ripples on a pond.

Waves are the same motion as snakes, but instead of the snake facing forwards wiggling side to side, point the head of the snake to one side, and make it wiggle up and down.

Waves are not pictured, if you want to practise them turn the book on its side and go back and repeat the Snakes lesson 9.

In some positions, you may find it easier to make your waves with the fingertips of each hand touching in the middle of the Snake, so that your wrists are at the head and tail of the Snake.

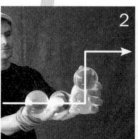

Donnie Darko Snake

If you've seen the film and can make good snakes, then this daft idea for a visual gag might appeal to you.

Donnie Darko:

"Every living thing follows along a set path. And if you could see your path or channel, then you could see into the future, right? Like err... that's a form of time travel."

With the back of the train/snake touching your chest, stand up and walk around to follow the snake! This looks better with a longer 5 ball snake.

5 Ball Snakes

The shorter 4 ball snake is far more versatile and expressive, but the extra length created by adding a ball between the hands makes it visually more elegant.

The extra ball is held between your fingertips of the back hand, and the heel of the front hand.

6 Ball Snakes

If you can hold 3 balls in a line in each hand, a 6 ball snake is possible and looks brilliant. However, this is very hard, and nowhere near as expressive as a 4 ball snake. In Contact, more is not always better.

3D Snakes

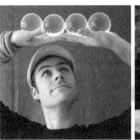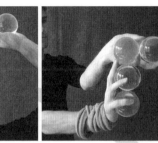

Get very three-dimensional with your snakes and trains, including large movements like Curls.

Helical Snakes Workshop

The Concept

This workshop gives an introduction to the three basic helical snake concepts.

Helical Snakes are the source of some of the hardest moves in Multiball Contact. Regular snakes are very difficult - Helical Snakes are stupidly difficult. They require a silly amount of practice to get into control, and can look rubbish unless they are presented very cleanly.

But what the heck, they rock!

Regular snakes travel in the shape of a sine wave, the wave motion travelling along the snake is two-dimensional (2D).

Helical Snake

A helical snake, as the name suggests follows the path of a helix in three dimensions.

This helix can be constructed from 2 sine waves, one going up/down and the other in/out of the page. So, helical snakes are a true 3D development of the 2D Snake.

Sine Wave
Regular Snake

Helix
Helical Snake

Helical Snake Curls

These Helical Snake Curls are the easiest of the three Helical Snakes shown here. Our top scientists at The Ministry of Manipulation have been working day and night to develop a learning method to simplify this move!

Two-handed bottle curls

Put your balls down for a moment and go and get an empty plastic bottle.

Start by holding the bottle up above your head as shown in the picture below.

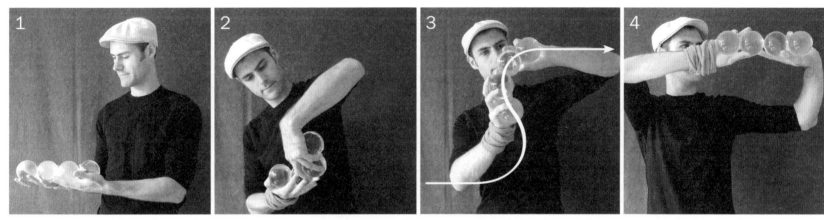

1 to 2 show the entry, and 3 to 4 show the exit from Helical Snake Curls, with a small section of the helix motion (2 to 3) in the middle

Throughout this bottle exercise, both hands should keep the same grip on the bottle with the tips of the thumbs touching and also the tips of the index fingers touching.

Make two handed curls (following the arrow in the picture- left). The bottle, being somewhat like a dead snake, does not curve around the helix. Keep your hands under the bottle and picture the helix motion. There should be a position at the bottom where your fingers are almost touching your belly.

Helical Snake Curls with 4 balls
Repeat the bottle exercise whilst holding 4 balls. This should be smoother, as the balls can flex to follow the path of the helix. Make sure you keep the balls in contact with their neighbours.

Entry and exit into Helical Snakes
Try the sequence 1 to 4 above. On the entry (1-2), palmspin the trailing hand. On the exit from the helix, palmspin the leading hand (3-4).

Try these variations
○ The reverse of above (4-1) and the mirror image of above (start on other side).
○ Putting a few of the Helical Snake Curls between your entry and exit.
○ Starting low to the floor, and climbing up two levels (e.g. 1,2,3,2,3,4) instead of just one level.
○ Start in position 1, climb up a helix on your right side (1-4), run horizontally at the top, then make the mirror image of the movement to descend on left side, finishing in the mirror image of 1.

Helical Snakes

The process of learning this motion is very similar to the basic snake in Lesson 9. The difference being that with a Helical Snake the balls move in semi-circles up and over, rather than along the horizontal lines of a basic Snake.

1 Start with 4 balls in a line. The line should be horizontal, and slightly pointing to the left side (as shown in figure 1). Throughout the motion, every ball should stay in contact with its neighbours. Start the first ball moving up and to the right, in a semi-circular motion.

2 The first ball completes a half circle to the side, finishing at the same height as the other balls. This makes position 3, the same "L" shape that appeared as the starting position for the snake lesson (Lesson 9, page 50).

3-4 The second ball makes a half circle to the side, staying in touch with both of its neighbours.

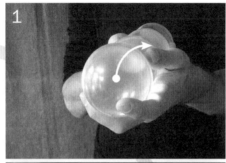

5-6 The third ball makes a half circle to the side.

7-8 The fourth ball makes a half circle to the side. Don't let the back ball get lazy - it should move the same amount as the other three in order to complete the effect.

9 Finish in a clean straight line half a ball width to the right side of the starting position. Repeat from figure 1.

Clean it up

Practise this until it is really clean. Take care to make each ball move the same amount, and on an even rhythm. A difficult part of this motion is to ensure that the lines are clean and that the balls are all at the same horizontal height when stationary - I can't emphasise enough how important this is to the visual effect.

As with regular Snakes, to make this movement into a flowing Helical Snake, start each ball moving before the previous ball has finished.

Helix variations

There are about eleventy gazillion variations of this Helical Snake motion to explore. Here are some ideas to get you started...

Reverse: This movement can be started with the front **or** the back ball of the snake.

Bottom Half: Each semi-circle can be carried up and over the snake as shown, or alternatively, down and underneath the snake. So each ball would make a semi-circle downwards and anti-clockwise.

Full Circles: The motions above really only make half a helix. By combining them it is possible to make full helix motions. A good combination is first the top half (1-9) as shown in the photos, followed by one helical snake bottom half **starting with the back ball**, to return you to position 1.

Vertical: Same motion but in a vertical axis - with the snake pointing upwards instead of forwards. You may find this easier if you open the snake up so that the balls are separated.

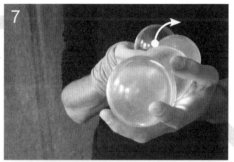

Helical Train

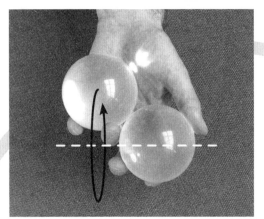

This drill will help you develop the motor skills needed for helical trains

First, practise the drill exercise pictured above. Hold 1 ball isolated and make vertical circles with the other ball. The balls should stay in contact throughout the motion.

Now swap so that the first ball is making vertical circles and the second is held isolated. The circles should be the same size as those you made with the first ball.

Practise the hell out of this drill with either hand until they are really clean. They are the building blocks for making helical trains.

Helical Trains
Imagine a helix running sideways in front of your body. Then try to make your helical snake follow this path (figures 1-5).

Helical trains are a real mind mangler - good luck, this motion is very difficult. It will take hours of intense concentration to get these clean enough so your audience can see the snake gliding along the path that you have visualised.

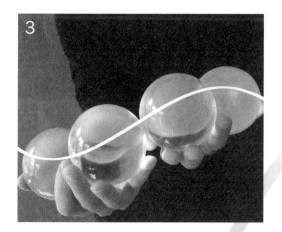

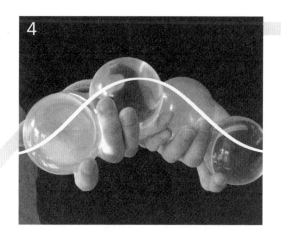

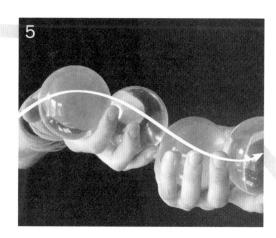

3D Helical Snakes...

There is a lot of uncharted territory to explore here - intricate and complex paths through space, with helices everywhere. It's a lot of work, but can be immensely rewarding to imagine a line through space and then take your snake on a journey along it.

5 Ball Contact

Five balls is a fantastic number for Contact. There is a lot of material to be explored with 5 balls, especially the 5 ball pyramid shape.

At this point in the book, you possibly only own 4 balls. Let this section inspire you to pay a visit to your local juggling shop and treat yourself to a new acrylic. While you're at the shop, you might want to buy a sixth ball too ... And a seventh (the flowers with seven are beautiful) ... But then, if you've got seven, you might as well get eight, so you can play with a pyramid in both hands ... And then there's nine balls!

If you can palmspin a 4 ball pyramid, you will find that most of this 5 ball Contact is well within your grasp. It's harder, but not a lot harder, and it will open up new possibilities in your manipulation.

A good way to start getting to grips with 5 balls is to repeat Lesson 5: Holding a Pyramid, with an extra ball - a 5 ball pyramid (a 4 ball square base with the fifth ball on top).

Flat Top Rocket [1.4]

This shape and movement is the same as the 4 ball rocket in Lesson 5, Exercise 5.4, with one extra ball.

Just like the 4 ball rocket, you can flat spin the top 4 balls.

The "[1.4]" in the title is Morphing Notation, for an explanation see Appendix 4.

5 Ball Flat Palmspinning

Palmspinning 3 balls in one hand and 2 in the other is very unbalanced. Instead, bring your hands together and play with 5 ball in two hands either in loops or in a cascade.

A 5 ball palmspinning cascade is a lot like the 3 ball in two hands cascade in Lesson 14, but with the balls not separated.

Starting with 2 balls in one hand and 3 in the other, palmspin both hands rolling inwards. Pass every ball across to the other hand as it comes to the centre. The passes will alternate, left, right, left, right, left, right, etc. The balls will travel around an infinity "∞" shape across your palms.

It is possible to learn to spin this pattern separated, and to have no clicks either, but it is **very** difficult. Most palmspinners perform it unseparated, with the balls hitting and try to minimise the impact and clicking sound.

Experiment with crossing and uncrossing your hands and adding thumb-lifts and pinky-lifts and you will find some great palmspinning variations with 5 balls.

5 Ball Pyramid Spinning in Two Hands

Palmspin a 5 ball pyramid with the square base held between two hands. Either aim to keep the base square (1), or let it pulse between (1) this square shape and (2) a rocket on its side [LR 1.3.1]. The pulsing version is less smooth, but is visually more beautiful.

Pyramid with a Sticky Ball

Palmspin a 4 ball pyramid in one hand. Hold 1 more ball in your other hand and keep it stuck to one face of the pyramid. Include thumb-lifts and pinky-lifts.

A very simple accompaniment to the sticky ball trick is to swap hands. Transfer the 3 balls that touch the sticky ball across to the hand that was holding the sticky ball, while keeping the whole thing smoothly rotating. The ball that was previously opposite the sticky ball becomes the new sticky ball.

Pyramid Ball Swap

1 A visually lovely move; start by spinning a 4 ball pyramid rolling outwards.

2-3 With one sweeping movement of the other hand, push the black ball into the base of the pyramid from the inside front.

4-5 Pull the clear ball it replaces out of the back of the pyramid base.

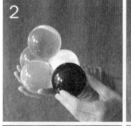

Rocket [1.3.1]

Make this shape by pushing 1 ball upwards from a flat top rocket.

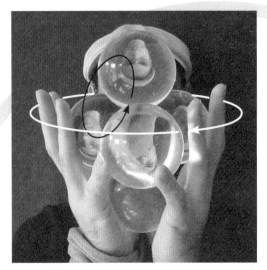

Spin the middle 3 balls (white arrow). This is simply a 4 ball rocket from Exercise 5.4 on page 36 with an extra ball on top. Concentrate on keeping the 3 middle balls in contact with each other, and as flat as possible.

It is possible to rotate any 3 of the top 4 balls in any direction, one alternative is shown by the black arrow. This is good training for learning to control lots of balls in formations.

Pyramid Rolling End Over End

Spin the pyramid as shown. For extra effect, isolate around the black ball.

A great variation: Rotate the pyramid until the black ball is directly underneath the other 4 and is still held in your fingertips.

Stop rotating and push the black ball vertically up through the middle, separating the other 4 balls to each side. Keep pushing up and re-close the square to make a pyramid and repeat (see also flipping a 6 ball rocket/diamond - which is the same trick with an extra ball - in the next section).

Cross Formation

Start by holding a pyramid in two hands, with your fingers underneath holding the 4 base balls and your thumbs holding the top (black) ball.

Next, tip your pyramid up so that the base is to the front, and the black ball is at the rear, closest to your body. Using your thumbs push the black ball forward into the middle, separating the 4 clear balls to make a cross.

" ...When the lowest type of men hear Tao, they laugh heartily at it.
Without the laugh, there is no Tao.
-Lao-tzu "

Multiball Contact
5 Ball Inspiration

Two Handed Curl

For a really evil move, try this: Hold a 5 ball pyramid with two hands - 2 balls of the base in either hand - and then try to make a two handed curl of this pyramid, without dropping the top ball.

Start the movement by pushing your right elbow around to the front, as you palmspin anticlockwise with your left hand.

See Lesson 7 which explains a two-handed curl with 4 balls in a line. This will help you understand the same movement with 4 balls in a square.

5 Balls in One Hand

Palmspinning 5 balls in one hand is hardcore Multiball Contact. It is the skill required to progress to 10 ball Contact.

5 Ball Breathing

Hold 5 balls in one hand, in a pyramid, and gently squeeze opposite corners to alternate between the two positions shown.

During this exercise focus on keeping all 4 clear balls in contact with the black ball.

This is not really a trick to perform, it's more of an exercise. It is good practice for starting to work with 5 in one hand, and for learning to do the next trick...

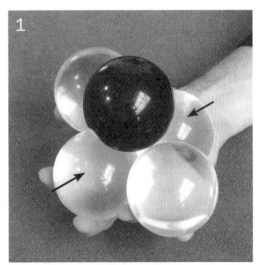

5 ball breathing

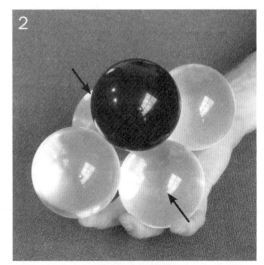

5 ball breathing

Palmspinning 5 in One Hand

ive ball pyramids with 3" balls are one of my favourite tricks, but they are **very** difficult, and put a great strain on the hand.

This is the trick that nearly forced me to quit Contact for good (see the warning box in the 10 ball section on page 126), and is the reason why this book preaches so much about warming up and looking after your hands.

Here are some tips that will help you learn this skill with a lot less hard work.

First, a Ninja Contact secret: spinning 5 in one hand is easier than spinning 4 balls in a flat square! The top ball helps to make the stack more stable.

Before trying to learn this movement, revise the methods used to teach palmspinning in Lessons 4, 11 and 12. All the hints and tips for palmspinning technique with any number of balls are given in these lessons.

After warming up throughly, practise your 4 ball pyramids until they are very clean and click free. Then work on making space in your hand with a 4 ball pyramid (like Exercise 11.2, page 59, only with 4 balls!).

It will also help you to increase the amount of space in your hand if you learn to palmspin 4 larger balls - if you have (or can borrow) them.

When you start working with a 5 ball pyramid, work through Lesson 5: Holding a Pyramid - only this time with 5 balls in a pyramid instead of 4. This will help you train your hand to hold the pyramid cleanly.

I'm not 100% convinced that it helpful for 5 ball pyramids to practice by using a lighter stage ball as the top of the pyramid. It has the big advantage of lighter weight, but I find that the extra friction disrupts the flow of base balls. Try it, you may find it helpful.

When you start spinning the 5 ball pyramid, use your other hand to help push it around.

Concentrate on keeping the base square. Stop it slipping into a diamond shape - the control you learned in the 5 ball breathing exercise on the last page will help with this.

Look after your hands - if you start getting any pain or discomfort, stop and take a break and cool down carefully.

When you get 5 ball palmspinning smooth with medium to large balls, well done, you have become a very skilful palmspinner!

6 Ball Contact

Six ball Contact is about symmetry. Its strength is palmspinning 3 balls in each hand. Adding Isolations to palmspinning makes 3 in each hand become magical - especially when you thumb-lift or pinky-lift the isolated ball.

Or you can then fly 2 triangles around your stage as 2 spaceships in formation. The two spaceships can then be joined together to create a rocket/diamond (page 109) which can be made to spin in every direction.

In order to start 6 balls you will need to have 3 ball palmspinning, thumb-lifts and pinky-lifts smooth in both hands in both directions.

For the formations it will help to have learned the 5 ball pyramid and rocket shapes first. The pyramid and rocket formations are 5 balls in **two** hands. You don't need to master 5 balls in **one** hand until you get to 9 ball formations.

6 Ball Mind Games

Three balls spinning in either hand with thumb-lifts and pinky-lifts. The hands can either mirror each other to show symmetry, or do the same thing in parallel.

The real potential here is that 3 balls in each hand allows you to isolate one ball in each hand and make a 6 ball version of Mind Games with Thumb-lifts and Pinky-lifts (see Lesson 8). As you start move your hands around your body more - this leads to the following trick: Spaceships.

4 ball Mind Games will help a lot with the coordination required for this.

Spaceships

The triangles you hold in each hand make aeroplanes or spaceships. 1 ball is the nose of the plane, the other 2 are the wings. Then you can make them dog-fight or fly them around in formation like a "6 ball Red Arrows" display team.

6 Ball Line Spin - Two lines

Flat line spins never feel smooth. Move... clunk... move... clunk... If you want to present this trick well, try to make the tray of balls as flat as possible and work hard to minimise clicking.

See also tray transfers (page 117).

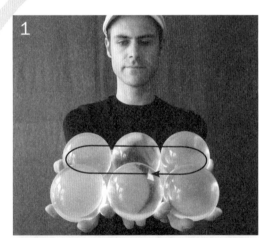

6 Ball Flower in Two Hands

A lovely shape to make, which can be rotated using two handed palmspinning.

6 Ball Torpedo

Using thumb-lifts you can make this whole shape rotate about an axis through the 2 end balls.

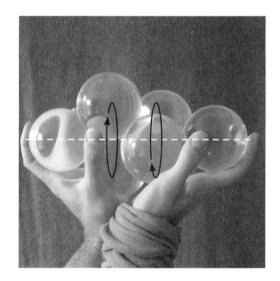

" Think of Nothing. When you start to think, that's when everything starts to fall. — Mr Om "

6 Ball Rocket/Diamond

Visually the most appealing formation in 6 balls is this Rocket held in a basket. There are a lot of ways it can be manipulated:

Spin it:
The easiest way to rotate this is to spin it around the vertical axis (black arrow below).

Also, it is possible to rotate any 3 or 4 of the upper balls in any direction (white arrows below show 3 of the possible 3 ball rotations).

Also, any of the rotations shown for the 7 ball flower (pages 114-115) are possible and easier with this rocket/diamond.

Flip it:
This is the same as the 5 ball pyramid rolling end over end (page 104).

Lower the rocket, keep the top pointing upwards by palmspining as you lower it. Then with your thumbs, reach up and hold the top ball between your thumb tips.

Lift the rocket back up to head height, as you lift, flip it over, so the top becomes the bottom (second picture below). With a bit more palmspinning you're back in the original basket position.

Curl it:
You can even make a two handed curl while holding this rocket. It is quite a strain to keep four square balls flat, but that is the detail which needs practice, to be able to present this trick well.

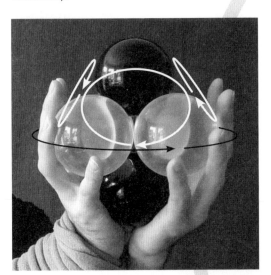

More 6 ball ideas....

Rotating and Non-Rotating Curls
See 8 ball curls in the 8 ball section and Lesson 7 - Curls.

6 Ball Flower in One Hand
See the section for people with "Small Balls" (page 133).

Formations & Morphing

Formations are about making and holding cool shapes with lots of balls, **Morphing** is changing between those shapes.

There are some simple formations with 4, 5, and 6 balls. The really juicy material arrives in the following sections with 7 to 11 balls.

The larger formations are impressive simply because of their massive size, but more balls are far more difficult and therefore more limiting in how they can be morphed.

There are several families of formations and morphing moves, with still more to be discovered:

- **Rockets/Diamonds:** 5 to 8 balls
- **Torpedoes:** Rockets on their side with 5 to 11 balls
- **Flowers:** With 6 and 7 balls
- **Bowls and Rings:** With 8 and 9 balls

Formation Notation

Next to the names of many of the formations in this book, you will find some numbers - a geeky notation for formations. Like this:

"Hourglass [3.1.3]"

If you really get into exploring formations, the notation will make a lot of sense and may even help! You'll find an explanation for it in Appendix 4: Formation Notation (page 149).

If on the other hand you're a right-thinking sensible ball manipulator, I recommend you shake your head, mumble something like: *"Bloody geeks, this is worse than siteswap,"* and move on to the next chapter. Personally I'm a manipulation super-geek, and proud of it.

Even Bigger Formations

This book goes up to 11 balls, but that's not the limit of Contact, late at night, when contact jugglers start getting silly, they start helping each other to make and hold ludicrous formations with 13, 16, or even 20 balls! These are just a bit of fun to do, and they look cool, until they cascade onto the floor in a shower of acrylic balls. See the "More Than 11 Balls?" section for more inspiration (page 132).

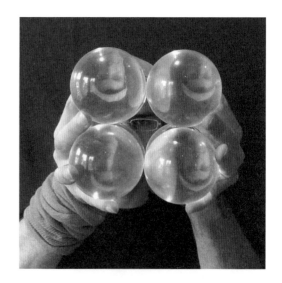

This is where multiball really starts hotting up, with the arrival of some of the best of formations and morphing possibilities including the 7 ball flowers on the next page.

Due to the odd number, 7 balls, is not the best for classic palmspinning (try 6 or 8 balls for that), but with such a wealth of great morphing material and formations to be played with, 7 ball Contact is definitely one of the most exciting areas to explore.

Before attempting this 7 ball material, you will need to be comfortable with 4 ball pyramid palmspinning, thumb-lifts and pinky-lifts, in either hand and either direction.

It will also help to have practised many moves with 5 and 6 balls.

Hourglass [3.1.3]

The hourglass is a 4 ball palmspinning pyramid with 3 balls held upside down on the top.

The bottom 3 balls are palmspinning, the top 3 balls are held and are not spinning.

For bonus style points, move this around and flip it upside down.

7 Ball Flat Line Spin

Flat line spins never feel smooth, nonetheless they can look awesome - especially if you isolate one of the balls!

To present this trick at its best, make the tray of 7 balls as flat as possible, minimise clicking and keep to an even rhythm.

Learn the easier 6 ball Line Spin first (page 108). When you have 7 balls solid, you can add 2 more balls on top for a difficult 9 ball palmspinning move - Tray Transfers (page 123).

7 Ball Moschen Transfer

This move was first performed by Michael Moschen in his pioneering routine "Light" - the first documented performance of crystal ball manipulation. Light is a fantastic routine, and is essential viewing for all multiball manipulators. (See Appendix 6.)

First practise this simplified version:

1 Start with 7 balls, 3 balls in the left hand and a 4 ball pyramid in the right. For the moment, ignore step 2, and lower your left hand.

3&4 Thumb-lift the pyramid to transfer the top ball back and forth between your hands.

Now try the whole transfer:
Adding step 2, a pinky-lift, to the previous exercise.

1 Start with 7 balls, 3 balls in your left hand and a 4 ball pyramid in your right.

2 Start to pinky-lift the 3 balls in your left hand, bringing the top ball in to touch the black ball. To make this work smoothly isolate around the black ball as you pinky-lift. Then start to thumb-lift the pyramid...

3 ... as you complete the thumb-lift of the pyramid transfer the black ball across to the left hand.

4 You should finish in the mirror image of the starting position.

Smoothing it out:
Start by palmspinning both hands clockwise, (not simply holding), blend all the movements together. Keep the motion of the balls smooth and constant. Blend the end of the transfer into flat anti-clockwise palmspinning (both hands). Then repeat on the other side.

There will be some clicking in this move - your aim is to try and minimise this as much as possible.

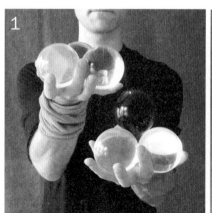
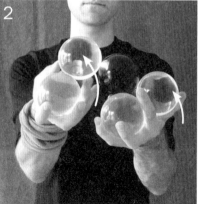

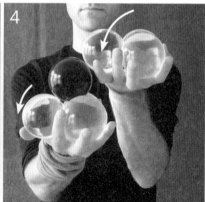

" It's not just rolling balls around. "
- Emanuele

Multiball Contact
7 Ball Inspiration

7 Ball Flowers & Morphing

Rolling W

"W" [4.3]

The "W" is one of the easiest formations to make, and is a starting point for many of the other formations with 7 balls.

Begin with 3 balls in one hand and a 4 ball pyramid in the other, both held with a point towards the outside. Push your hands together and lift up the balls on either side to form a W shape in a basket.

Think of this formation as two 3 ball triangles - one in each hand, holding the black ball between them.

1 Lower the W-shape down in front of you by rotating your hands so that your little fingers touch. Hold the two triangles - without palmspinning. This should "roll" the triangles around the W, bringing the 2 top clear balls inward to the front base of the formation.

2 This is the tricky bit. Look at the formation - you will see there are 4 balls in a square which form the bottom layer. Lift the W back up to the basket position in front of your face. As you do, palmspin each triangle (inwards) to keep those 4 balls flat at the bottom of the stack.

3 This should bring you back to the starting position, with the clear balls all rotated one position forwards around their triangles. Repeat.

W Rotating Another Way [2.5]

Continuously rotate the front 5 balls! Or alternatively, hold this up in a basket and rotate the top 5 balls to make a mutant-twin version of 4 ball rockets.

7 Ball Flat Flower

To make this shape, lower it straight out of W, separating the 4 bottom balls to the front and rear.

Tip this flower slightly forward to show the audience. This will allow you to support the back 2 balls with your wrists.

With 3" balls this is too large to palmspin, but it is possible with smaller balls.

7 Ball Flower [1.5.1]

This 7 ball flower formation is fantastic - it has a wealth of possibilities. Form it in one movement from W by palmspinning a fraction of a rotation with 1 hand to lower 1 of the 4 bottom balls.

This is the big sister of the 6 ball Rocket/ Diamond (page 109).

It can be held with the points of the flower pointing up-down, pointing front-to-back or pointing side-to-side as a torpedo.

Side to side

The flower can be rotated in any direction...
Some of these are not easy!

Front to back

In each of these three positions the flower can be rotated in three directions, about the x-axis, y-axis or z-axis, although some of these are very difficult!

It is great to have so much freedom to manipulate a formation in any direction.

More 7 ball...

There are many different morphings to be explored with 7 balls - how to get from any formation to any other, via the most elegant path.

The inspiration sections on 4, 6 and 8 balls will give you some clues to help explore 7 ball formations and moves that are not shown in this book.

8 Ball Contact

For many years 8 balls was considered to be the pinnacle of multiball contact. There is a vast range of great palmspinning and formations to explore with 8 balls, taking it far beyond what is given in this book.

Rotating the 8 ball torpedo is one of the best moves in Contact. It looks great, and it's not as difficult as you might first think.

Before starting with 8 balls you will need to be able to palmspin 4 balls in either hand.

It's a big step up from being able to spin a pyramid in either hand, to two pyramids at the same time. Practising 5, 6 and 7 ball Contact will help make that journey easier and more fun.

Thumb-lifts and pinky-lifts are essential for all the formations and morphing in this section.

If you are having trouble learning the formations, ask a friend to help you make and hold the shape, and with picking up the drops.

Picking Up 8 Acrylics

1 Load 4 balls into your left hand in a pyramid.

2 Place a fifth ball in the left hand. Either as shown below, held by ring and little fingers or alternatively balanced on your wrist leaning against the back of the pyramid.

3 Pick up another 3 balls in your empty hand.

4 Transfer the fifth ball across to form the top ball of the second pyramid (below).

Double Pyramids

The classic palmspinning trick. Although this is not the easiest move with 8 balls, I recommend you start your 8 ball manipulation by learning to work with 2 pyramids: palmspinning with either hand, in either direction, and thumb-lifts and pinky-lifts. This will help you with the other 8 ball tricks.

Try not to get into the habit of spinning pyramids in only one position. They're a lot more exciting to watch when they are smoothly moved around in all directions.

When you can make 50 shifts in any rotation without making a single click, then you have mastered palmspinning.

By adding isolations to one ball in each pyramid, a fantastic visual effect is possible - which is amplified if you thumb-lift or pinky-lift the isolated ball (difficulty: 5).

Curls & Spinning Curls

Curls are explained in Lesson 7. Non-rotating curls (holding, not palmspinning) are one of the easiest things to do with 8 balls. But be careful, there's a risk of those top balls falling off and landing on you.

Conversely, curls whilst palmspinning are one of the hardest 8 ball manipulations. Anyone who can do these has put in a lot of hours of practice.

A special case of rotating curls is "zeroing", which isolates the rotation of the pyramid. To zero palmspin in the opposite direction to the curl, keeping the orientation of the stack the same (the same ball at the front) throughout the whole motion. This is a very difficult trick, but well worth the effort for the visual effect.

Tray Transfers [6.2]

While palmspinning both hands clockwise, gently bring two pyramids together. Make one transfer, swapping 2 bottom balls, and then pull the stacks apart, back to two spinning pyramids.

When you have individual tray transfers working smoothly, build up to two transfers in a row, then three transfers, and finally continuous tray transfers as pictured left. The 6 clear balls on the bottom form a tray which is continuously spinning, with the 2 black balls stationary on the top.

To make this difficult movement easier to learn, first practise these exercises:

- Practise without the top balls (6 ball two line spin, page 108).

- Practise with only 1 ball on top first (7 balls total) and concentrate on keeping the tray clean. All your attention will be on the back middle ball - this is the troublesome one, as the weight of the balls on top will try to push it off your hands.

8 Ball Torpedo [LR 1.3.3.1]

This is an awesome 8 ball trick which is not as difficult as it might look.

Lift two pyramids up in front of your face, and then push them together in the middle. This can be rotated forwards or backwards. Good 4 ball thumb- and pinky-lifts are essential for this rotation.

Syncro Torpedo [LR 1.3-3.1]

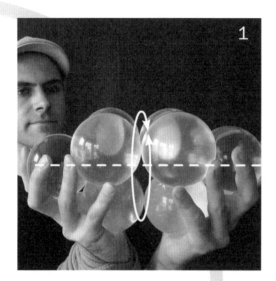

This torpedo can be rotated in many directions forwards and backwards.

The most obvious rotation is shown above (1). Think of this formation as two pyramids, one controlled by each hand.

An alternative and more complex movement is to rotate each of the two pyramids around the axes shown in picture 2.

They can only rotate one-third of a turn before they collide, reforming a syncro

torpedo (with the side balls now touching at the front and the back balls now at the sides).

Rotating a small amount (one third of a turn) as shown in picture 1 will return you to the position shown in picture 2: with 4 balls square at the front.

To repeat the process:
... one-third turn (2)... one-third turn (1)... one-third turn (2)... one-third turn (1)... etc

8 Ball Ring

1&2 From a syncro torpedo, flat rotate a little (1) to form the intermediate position (2).

3 Squeeze together and push up to form the 8 ball ring (3).

8 Ball Ring

Hint: The top two balls are tricky to balance. To make this easier to practise you could replace them with 2 sticky stage balls.

8 Ball Flat Palmspinning

Separating 8 balls in half and spinning four flat in each hand is harder that spinning 10 balls in two 5 ball pyramids!

8 Ball Flat Linespin

An easier flat palmspinning trick is to join your hands and spin 8 balls in two lines. This, like any line spin, feels very lumpy, and can't be done silently. Learn the 7 ball flat line spin first.

One-Four-Three [1.4.3]

There are many ways into and out of this shape. One option is by pushing up one of the end balls in an 8 ball Torpedo while slightly tipping the remaining 7 balls.

Bowl [2.6ring]

Opening the top of a syncro torpedo will make a bowl shape. Form the bowl in the upright position, then tip it forward (as shown below) to show to the audience.

Bowl Tipped Forward

Cube [4.4]

Press in the left and right sides of an 8 ball ring to make two flat diamond shapes next to each other. Then gently lower the diamonds into two squares, forming this cube.

Don't squeeze a cube too hard - it's highly unstable and will explode!

Rocket Demon [1.3.3.1]

There are many ways into this. Tipping over [1.4.3] then pushing a ball to the bottom is a good way to start.

A Rocket is a Torpedo, tipped vertically

By the same theme, the syncro demon [1.3-3.1] is also possible.

Celestial Demon [1.3,3,1]

This is a very difficult formation to make, and even harder to get out of elegantly. Here it is shown tipped forwards to show the top view; it is normally formed vertically

like the Rocket Demon. It has a great shape when viewed from the front.

This same Demon can be formed upside down, with the three horns pointing downwards.

See Appendix 4: Morphing Notation for more diagrams of Demons (page 149).

"Demons" have this name because of their difficulty - they're such "demons" to make. This Celestial Demon haunted me for months, spending hours working out how to make it, and then forgetting again and again... Arrrgh, what a nightmare. All I could remember is that it can be formed in one movement from one of the common 8 ball formations.

More Ideas With 8 Balls

The inspiration sections on 4, 6 and 7 balls will give you some hints as to formations and moves that are missing from this chapter.

There is lots more to be explored with 8 ball formations and different elegant morphings.

For a bit of fun have a look at "Interstitial Atoms" in the Small Balls section (page 135).

9 Ball Contact

Due to the asymmetry, 9 ball Contact doesn't offer many great palmspinning options; but like 7 balls, it does have some fantastic formations.

Realistically, in order to get anywhere with 9 ball Contact you need to be comfortable palmspinning 5 balls in either hand.

Picking Up 9 – Easy Way

Pick up 8 balls as in the previous chapter. Then, using your little fingers to help, ease the ninth ball up between your hands into a low torpedo (see pictures below). It's easy, but not the most elegant way to do it.

1

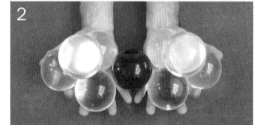

2

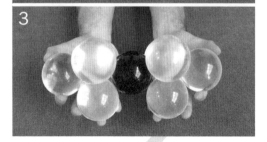

3

Picking Up 9 – With Wrist

1 Place 5 balls in your right hand in a square based pyramid.

1, 2 & 3

2 Place the sixth ball on your wrist, leaning against the back 2 balls in the pyramid.

4

9 Ball Palmspinning

3 Pick up 3 balls in the left hand (no worries so far).

4 Roll the ball from the right wrist onto the top of the 3 balls in the right hand to form a pyramid ...

5 ... and you're ready to palmspin.

Picking Up 9 – The Scoop

The smoothest, and also the hardest way to pick up 9 balls. Good practice for picking up 10 and 11 balls though. See the "Scoop" and the "Double Scoop" explained with photos in the 10 ball section (page 126).

Palmspinning 4 balls in one hand and 5 in the other is a bit unbalanced - the solution is to keep the extra ball frequently swapping between your two hands.

Tray Transfers with Two Pyramids [7.2]

Learn the 8 ball tray transfer and the 7 ball flat line spin first.

Palmspin both hands in the same direction, clockwise or anticlockwise, and you can make a move just like an 8 ball tray transfer, with an extra ball (pictured on the right).

Alternatively have both hands spinning outwards (or inwards) and regularly swap balls in the middle. This makes a move a bit like the "5 ball flat cascade", but with a lot of extra balls.

9 Ball Formations

9 Ball Torpedo [LR 1.3.1.3.1]

Bring your hands together to form the torpedo on a tray, then lift it up to the basket position (figure 2).

Full Bowl [2.7]

Push the ends of the Torpedo inwards to make this full bowl (pictured below). Yes, there are 2 more balls in the picture, - behind the black ball. This is much like the 8 ball (empty) bowl on page 120. Form and melt the bowl in the vertical position, with the black ball on top (in the bowl), but tip it forward to show the flower shape to the audience as shown below.

Torpedo With a Ball on Top

Squeeze the front and back of the Full Bowl and slightly separate the 2 side balls, as shown by the black arrows in the picture below. This will lift the centre ball.

You need to move 7 balls simultaneously to make this torpedo with a ball on top!

Tie

1 From the Torpedo with a Ball on Top: Push the 2 end balls up onto the top of the formation to make the intermediate position (2).

2 Next, separate the middle layer to lower the centre ball into position and push the 2 top balls inwards...

3 ...to make the formation "Tie". Note the equal gap between the "wings" both top and bottom.

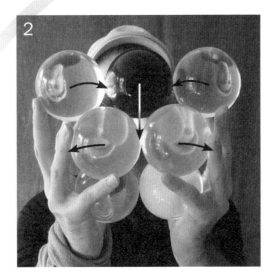

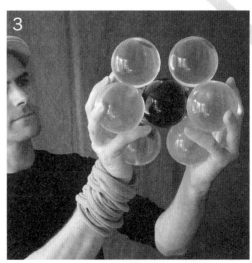

"The Force is with you, young Skywalker... but you are not a Jedi yet."

Ten ball Contact is great for formations and for palmspinning. Those 5 ball pyramids in each hand are big and heavy, making a big step up in difficulty from 8 to 10 balls.

The key is to stay relaxed. Too much tension or too much pressure will cause those big formations to explode, firing acrylics all over the room.

Good luck!

> **WARNING:** Contact juggling with high numbers of balls can be a quick route to damaged tendons in the hands and wrists or RSI (Repetitive Strain Injury). If you're going to work on 10 balls, please be very careful, take each progression very gently and slowly, and warm up before you start.
>
> If you get any ache or discomfort please take a break. Go back a step and train more with fewer or smaller balls.

Picking up 10 – Scoop

1 Place 5 balls in your left hand in a square based pyramid.

2 Place the sixth ball on the front of the stack, supported by your ring finger as shown in the picture.

Alternatively you may find it easier to place the sixth ball on the wrist of your left hand leaning against the 2 back balls of the 5 ball stack (see Picking Up 9 - With Wrist, page 122).

3 Pick up 3 balls in your right hand. Shift these balls towards the back of your palm.

4 With your right hand make a fork with your index finger and middle finger. Open up a gap between the 2 front balls in the palm, making room for a fourth ball.

See also pictures 1 and 2 opposite, which show the scoop action.

2, 4 & 5

6

Picking up 10 – Double Scoop

5 Scoop along the floor, slowly and gently until you have a flat four in your right hand. This is easier on a soft surface where the ball does not roll. It may help to push this last ball against your other hand to make the scoop.

6 Roll the black ball, from the left hand onto the top of the right hand - and now you're ready to go with 10 ball palmspinning.

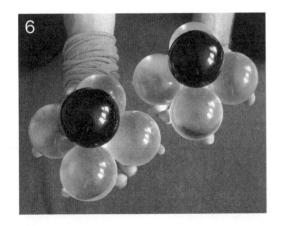

This is the harder, but more elegant way of picking up 10 balls. You will find this very difficult if the balls are resting on a hard surface. Learn it on a rug or carpet.

1 Pick up 8 balls, 5 in your left hand, 3 in the right. Move the 3 balls in your right hand into the back of your palm, and with your right hand make a fork with the index finger and middle finger. Open up a gap between the 2 front balls in the palm.

2 Scoop a fourth ball into your right hand, and lift it up to into a 4 ball pyramid.

3 Slightly open a gap between the front 2 balls again and make a fork by separating your ring and index fingers.

4 Scoop up the final ball into the fork to complete the 5 ball pyramid.

This **is** possible... honestly!

127

Non-Rotating Curls

Surprisingly, these are easier with 10 balls than with 8, because of the extra stability of the 5 ball pyramids. However, rotating curls with 10 balls are insanely difficult.

10 Ball Breathing

You can do 5 ball breathing (page 105) with both hands. This is a good first exercise for learning to control so many balls, and a good first step to ease you into palmspinning 10 balls.

10 Ball Palmspinning

10 Ball Double Pyramids

Five ball pyramids (page 106) with both hands. Go for it! But do be careful of the risk of hand damage. Warm up and be aware of your posture and breathing.

Both hands in both directions of course!

10 Ball Wrist Balance

Squeeze the back ball out of the stack and hold it balanced on your wrist or roll it along the forearm to the elbow crease. Then work with the 4 ball stack left in your hand.

The wrist balance is a little bit tricky as the tendons in the wrist will move as you palmspin, which will upset the balance of the ball.

10 Ball Formations

Here are a few lovely formations with 10 balls to get you started. If you've worked through all the 8 and 9 ball formations, then little instruction should be necessary for these.

Staircase [Diagonal 2.2.2.2.2]

Start with two 5 ball pyramids, with the 2 black balls on the front outside corners of the pyramid bases. Then merge the two to make the formation shown below.

10 Ball Syncro Torpedo [LR 1.4-4.1]

Shift the higher hand down from the Staircase. There's an 8 ball cube held in the middle of this! Consequently, it tends to be a little unstable.

10 Ball Torpedo [LR 1.4.4.1]

Rotate one hand a third of a turn from the Syncro Torpedo to form the Torpedo (pictured below).

More 10 ball ideas...

Look in the Small Balls inspiration section at the three layer pyramid on page 134.

11 Ball Contact

Eleven balls Is the uncharted territory of Contact. Just managing to pick them up is an achievement!

When you've got your 10 ball Contact solid, you will find that all the following are possible to form an 11 ball sequence.

The sheer size and weight of eleven 76mm (3") acrylics is impressive. 11 ball contact is incredibly limiting, but heck...Why not?

Picking Up 11 Balls

Combining the two methods described for picking up 10 balls (pages 126 and 127) will allow you to pick up eleven 3" acrylics.

1 Put 6 balls in one hand, a 5 ball pyramid with a sixth ball held on the front with your middle or ring finger.

2 Then make a double scoop to lift 5 into the other hand. Now you've got 11 balls off the floor and into your hands.

3 Bring the hands together squeezing the sixth ball between the two pyramids. Palmspin both hands a quarter turn into the following full tray position.

Full Tray [8.3]

Is it possible to spin or curl this full tray? Maybe, who knows? Not by me,...yet.

Halite [LR 1.4.1.4.1]

This is my favourite 11 ball trick. It is morphed in one movement from the previous formation.

Note: To make this halite as shown, the black balls on either side of the Full Tray on the previous page need to have started in different positions. That is, in the front bottom outside corners of the full tray.

This formation was found as a result of studying the way that atoms pack in crystals.

It takes its name and its inspiration from sodium chloride - a mineral more commonly known as rock salt.

This formation represents the chloride atoms in 2 unit cells of a face centred cubic halite crystal lattice. The shape forms two octahedral holes. In rock salt the sodium atoms fit inside these octahedral holes formed by the chlorine atoms (*See top of page).

11 Ball Bridge

Halite can be pressed up and morphed into this:

Note: The 2 lower black balls would be at the extreme side positions if made from the Halite shown in the previous picture.

From here, you can lower back down to Full Tray, the starting position, and make all of this section into a nice sequence.

More Than 11 Balls?

Using the Contact Jugglers standard ball size of 3" acrylics, 11 balls seems to be the maximum limit at the moment.

So right now if you want to go beyond 11, you're going to have to downsize your balls, or get a friend to help you.

There is no doubt that soon someone will come along with giant hands who can palmspin 6 balls in each hand and construct never before dreamed of formations.

For me the most difficult material is with 1, 2, 4 or 10 balls. The most enjoyable is with 1, 3, 4, 5, 7 and 8 balls. More balls tend to provide more constraints rather than more freedom to be creative and expressive.

Get a Friend to Help

A good late night game for Contact manipulators is to try to hold stupidly large formations. These are made with the help of other people placing balls on top.

13 Ball torpedo {1.5.1.5.1}

A 13 ball Torpedo, a 10 ball 3 layer pyramid [6.3.1] and an 11 ball 3 layer pyramid [7.3.1] can all be formed in two hands - with help of course!

Multi Person Formations

Another late night Contact game is to experiment with creating formations held using more than two hands.

With three hands from three different people using 3" balls it is possible to build and hold a 4 layer pyramid with 20 balls [10.6.3.1].

I'm pictured here with Ryan from Canada (centre) and Pich from France (right), late at night at the British Juggling Convention.

Some folk like to use little tiny balls of about 44 - 57mm (1.75 – 2.25") diameter for their multiball contact. Some use little metal Chinese medicine balls, often called Baoding balls after the region in China where they are manufactured (see Appendix 1, page 142).

Smaller balls are less stable, and less smooth in their motion. But they do allow you to experiment with a greater number of balls, and can be more useful for some magic tricks.

Real Men Have Large Balls

Good Contact is all about smoothness and presentation. The larger the balls you work with, the smoother and the more visual your Contact becomes.

For example: **three** 50mm (2") balls are required to get the same volume and visual impact as **two** 68mm (2.5") balls, and as only **one** 76mm (3") acrylic.

And it takes at least six 2" balls to have the same volume and the same visual size as just one 4" acrylic.

Separated Flat 4

There are unconfirmed reports that it is possible to palmspin 4 balls separated flat in one hand using 50mm (2") balls. My guess is that this is very difficult.

Palmspinning 6 Ball Flower in One Hand

With smallish balls, 50-63mm (2 to 2.5") diameter, palmspinning a 6 ball flower in one hand is quite manageable.

Palmspinning Flat 7 Flower in One Hand

With small - 50mm or 2" diameter balls it is even possible to palmspin 7 balls in one hand.

10 Ball Three Layer Pyramid

With two hands and 50mm (2") balls you can work with a 10 ball three layer pyramid [6.3.1] as if it were a 4 ball pyramid, using all the moves and transfers from Lesson 5.

Palmspinning these three layer pyramids is beyond me. I know of no-one who can do it, although I suspect it may be possible.

Palmspinning this three layer pyramid is beyond me ...

... although rotating this rocket is quite possible.

11 Ball Three Layer Pyramid

There is room on the top of the flat 7 Flower in one hand (previous page) for another 4 balls in a pyramid. Theoretically it would be possible to palmspin this 11 ball three layer flower based pyramid.

An article by Eva and Wolfram Wirbelwind in Kascade magazine (June 1994, Issue 34) suggests that a good way to make this 11 ball pyramid is to glue the top four balls together.

Interstitial Atoms

This would make it a lot easier to perform this very visual trick on stage, but for manipulation purists, this "magic effect" seems to be a little bit like cheating.

It's good to have dreams. 22 ball palmspinning (without glue) is something I would like to see ... one day.

How hard would this be? I don't know! As far as I know, no-one has ever done it. It is harder than **very** hard. I've never managed to spin more than 9 in either hand (in a flat 7 with 2 more balls on top).

An ingenious idea from Emanuele is that little tiny balls can be fitted into the gaps in your formations.

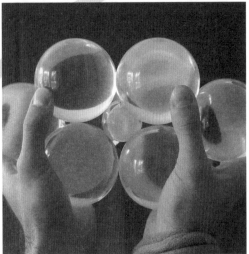

A 40mm acrylic will fit into the middle of an 8 ball Syncro Torpedo, as shown above and the formation can still be rotated. A 30mm acrylic can fit into the centre of an 8 ball Torpedo made with 3" balls (page 118).

The End of the Inspiration Section. From here onward, you make your own ideas.

"The question is often asked me, how to become a juggler. There is only one way, and one rule. It applies to everything else equally well, and that is: Whatever you make up your mind to do, stick to it until it is done. I have found it works very well."   - Paul Cinquevalli (1859 - 1918)

Cinquevalli, "The Human Billiard Table" wore a green felt jacket with billiard "pockets" sewn onto it. He would manipulate billiard balls over his body and land them in the pockets. The following is an extract from: The Greatest Juggler in the World, an article by William G. Fitzgerald The Strand Magazine, Vol XIII, Jan-June 1897.

"Briefly, he plays an orthodox, scientific game of billiards on his own sinewy person. The jacket is of real billiard cloth, with five beautifully-made pockets of cord and brass wire. The sixth "pocket" is the juggler's own right ear, and his forehead is "spot." His arms and knees serve as cushions, and wonderful cushions they are...."

"The game is a very miracle of neatness and skill. The balls fly into the air, cannon and then descend, only to glide hither and thither, in and out of the pockets, actuated only by a series of sharp jerks on the part of the player. "When the balls are moving over my back, I am guided only by the sense of touch." And marvellously delicate must that sense be, considering the relative lightness of the balls and the thickness of the green jacket and tights. The prettiest and most difficult move of all is from the low back pocket into one of the shoulder pockets. The ball doesn't seem to know where to go; it runs along hesitatingly, but at last it recognises its destination, and seeks it with a comical little spurt."

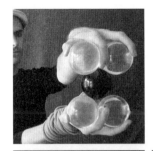

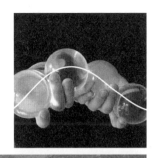

Appendices & Useful Information

Appendix 1: Balls

Which balls you use for Multiball Contact depends on the size of your hands and the size of your wallet.

This appendix explains the different ball options. Appendix 2 explains how to choose the correct size of balls for your hands.

Best for Quality

The quick answer is: For Multiball Contact, the best balls are Acrylics. 4 clear acrylic balls, 75mm (3") diameter will cost you about £100, €136 or US$112 (2006 prices). If you have small hands, use smaller balls - and they'll be cheaper too (see Appendix 2).

A cheaper option for a beginner is to buy 4 wooden balls. 4 wooden balls 75mm (3") diameter will cost you about: £20, €24 or US$24.
Again use smaller balls if you have small hands - Appendix 2.

Best Budget Option

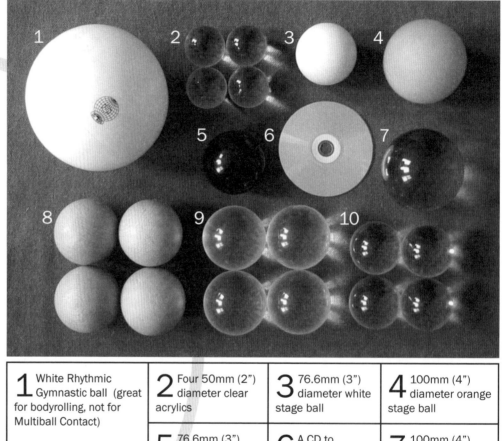

1 White Rhythmic Gymnastic ball (great for bodyrolling, not for Multiball Contact)	**2** Four 50mm (2") diameter clear acrylics	**3** 76.6mm (3") diameter white stage ball	**4** 100mm (4") diameter orange stage ball
	5 76.6mm (3") diameter black acrylic ball	**6** A CD to show scale (Lemonjelly again)	**7** 100mm (4") diameter clear acrylic ball
8 Four 76.6mm (3") diameter wooden balls	**9** Four 76.6mm (3") diameter clear acrylics		**10** Four 68mm (2.5") clear acrylics

Ball Options

For Multiball Contact and palmspinning you will need balls with a smooth and low friction surface.

The best choice
- Acrylic balls – The most beautiful and expensive option.

The alternatives (Page 142)
- Wooden balls – The cheapest option
- Transparent polycarbonate and polyester balls
- Silver metal balls and Chinese medicine balls

High friction balls (Page 143)
For separated palmspinning and for the 1 ball Contact in this book, you can use high friction balls such as: oranges, stage balls and silicone balls.

Acrylic Balls

Transparent acrylic balls are very beautiful, and have a smooth slippery low friction surface. They are the most popular ball for Multiball Contact.

Clear acrylic balls

Coloured & UV acrylics
In recent years, some manufacturers have started supplying coloured acrylics. These come in the following two flavours:

- Colour tinted acrylics which are still transparent so they still allow light through.

- Solid coloured acrylics which are not transparent, like giant snooker balls - such as the black balls shown in many photographs in this book.

Also a selection of UV acrylics have become available. My favourite set of acrylics are clear transparent spheres that glow like light blue bubbles in UV light and have a slight blue tint in sunlight.

Safety Warning

Sun + Acrylic Ball = Fire
Transparent balls can be dangerous. They are powerful lenses which focus the sun's rays and very quickly start fires that burn down houses and juggling shops. Always keep acrylics covered or out of direct sunlight when you are not using them.

On a sunny day, you can light a fire or a cigarette in a few seconds, and you will rapidly learn not to hold the ball stationary in direct sunlight as it can quickly burn your hands.

Care For Acrylic Balls

Acrylics can scratch and chip easily, these tips will help you make yours last longer.

Acrylic balls are pre-programmed at the factory to fly towards cups of tea, glass table tops, rocks and ornaments. Clear your training space of hard objects and preferably put a soft blanket over the floor.

Don't wear metal jewellery when handling acrylics, it can scratch the surface.

Get some good baggage to protect your balls. A lot of people keep their acrylics individually in socks! Separate bags for each ball will prevent them bumping and scratching against each other whilst you are carrying them around.

Keep your hands and balls clean - dirt and grit will scratch them.

It is possible to polish small scratches out of acrylic balls using "T-Cut", motorcycle visor polish or other plastic polishes such as the "Novus" plastic polish system. Some ball manufacturers offer to re-polish your balls for a small fee [£1] per ball plus postage costs.

Buying Good Acrylics

Not all acrylics are born equal; there is a huge variation in the quality of acrylics available today. It pays to shop around for quality as well as price. To make sure you get the best balls, apply these 5 tests:

1 Roundness
To check for roundness, put the ball on a flat, smooth, clean surface and spin it, look at the edges of the ball - any wobble and the ball is not round, reject it.

2 Good colour & transparency
Acrylic is not so much a material as a whole range of materials depending on what additives are in the plastic.

Clear acrylics are transparent and have a light transmission of about 96%, although this can be as low as 92% in poor quality balls. The remaining 4% has a colour, even the clearest transparent acrylic or glass has some slight hint of colour! The more expensive materials are generally the ones with the higher optical clarity. Manufacturers of cheaper balls save money by using a less transparent acrylic.

I have one cheap 4" which is a dull grey colour. Visually this does not have as strong a magical bubble effect as my other balls.

To test the colour and optical clarity, look carefully at an acrylic in daylight. Use your judgement and you should be able to pick out a good one. There is generally little variation across one batch.

Some manufacturers supply graded acrylics for precisely this reason with the higher quality (and higher price) balls being referred to as "Ultra-Clear Acrylics".

3 Check for scratches
Balls can get scratched during manufacture, distribution, or whilst waiting to find their correct owner in a juggling shop. Focus your eyes on the surface of the ball and check for heavy scratches.

> "There is geometry in the humming of the strings, there is music in the spacing of the spheres. - Pythagorus

4 Image quality

Acrylics are strong lenses - looking into one you can see a miniature image of your environment. This image is part of the magic of "crystal balls". Polishing is a time consuming process and some manufacturers save money by not polishing the balls to such a high standard. The surface will still be smooth, but the quality of the image in the ball will not be as good.

This will become very annoying when your isolations get accurate. The image in the ball will shimmer and move giving the perception that the ball is moving, even when it is perfectly isolated.

This is a tricky defect to detect. What you are looking at is the quality of the ball as a lens.

Here's a test: Hold a ball above this grid and look through the ball at the grid. Adjust the distance of the ball from the page so that the image of the grid is in focus. Gently rotate the ball as a held isolation. If the lines are distorted smoothly, the lens is good, if the

lines are very wobbly you may want to reject that ball. Try this test from a few angles.

There will always be some small wobbling of the lines, even in the best acrylics. The optical quality required to avoid this is usually only seen in camera and telescope lenses. But the question is whether there are any unacceptably large wobbles in the image.

5 Check for internal flaws

With low quality balls you may find internal bubbles, debris or imperfections that have been trapped in the acrylic during moulding. These are rare and usually very obvious, but it's worth checking - take a careful look into the ball for these.

Look through an acrylic held above this grid. Rotate the ball, if the lines are distorted smoothly, the lens is good, if the lines are very wobbly you may want to reject it. Try this test from a few angles.

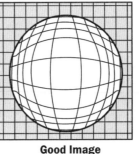

Good Image

Rough Image

Alternative Balls

Wooden Balls

Wooden balls make a good cheap alternative to acrylics for all contact juggling.

Mine are not very round, they have a natural feel and are uncoated plain wood. Softer, lighter, and with higher friction than acrylics, wooden balls make a lovely rich rubbing sound.

The higher friction than acrylics is noticeable when palmspinning, as it means that better technique and more effort is required to spin them smoothly. The friction can be reduced with the correct varnish.

Wooden balls are available in 50-100mm (2"-4") sizes from juggling shops and from architectural model making suppliers. Unvarnished 75mm (3") balls cost around £5, €5 or US$5 each (2006 prices).

Polyester & Polycarbonate Balls

At first glance these transparent balls may look identical to acrylics. When they are sometimes half the price of acrylics, they may look like a real bargain, but there are two major differences:

Polycarbonate and polyester do not have the same resistance to chemical attack as does acrylic. So sweat and grease from your hands tends to damage their surface, ageing polycarbonate and polyester balls more quickly than acrylics.

Clear polyester balls are nowhere near as transparent, and if you hold up a polyester ball next to an acrylic you will see that the polyester is a dull grey colour. Polycarbonate is better than polyester, but still not as optically clear as acrylic.

They also do not last as well, nor do they take as much abuse as acrylics. They may be half the price, but they will lose their appearance quickly. Buy acrylics if you can.

Silver Metal Balls

There are at least three different types, some are produced specifically for contact and have a weight similar to acrylics but with a silver mirrored surface. These are sold alongside acrylics and are very good for multiball - as good as acrylics.

Others are hollow and very light like stage balls, and are sold as ornaments. These

light balls dent very easily and are not very good for multiball as they don't have enough weight to give stability. They can be great for 1 ball Contact though.

The third type are Baoding balls, often which chime when played with. They go by many names, including: Chinese medicine balls, worry balls, stress balls, lotus balls, therapy balls, exercise balls, chiming balls, Qigong balls, meditation balls, iron balls, Baichi (valuable balls), Baodjan Chu (health balls). These can be used for multiball, but they are usually only available in sizes too small (up to 50 - 60mm/2 - 2.5") for most of the multiball style in this book.

Whichever ball you get, your contact juggling will improve much faster if the ball is orange coloured.

Multiball Contact
Appendix 1: Balls

High Friction Balls

High friction juggling balls such as stage balls are used in this book for palmspinning separated, and can be used for 1 ball contact - as indeed can almost anything round, such as oranges.

Stage Balls

A 75-100mm (3-4") soft stage ball is perfect for most people to start learning 1 ball Contact. There are also exercises in this book which require a high friction ball to match the size of your acrylics - for which a stage ball is ideal. Stage balls are often made from PVC which is environmentally one of the most polluting of plastics. Approximate cost £5-7, €9-10 or US$9-10

Hard or Soft: Stage balls are available either hard or soft. The soft ones are slightly squashy, which for most people makes them feel better and easier for 1 ball Contact.

Surface: Glossy stage balls tend to stick to the skin more which can be a little bit easier for some 1 ball moves - such as body rolling (a 1 ball technique not covered in this book). Peach finish balls are more slippery, but feel smoother. Either works fine - it's a matter of taste.

Oranges

Oranges are actually pretty good for palmspinning and most 1 ball Contact moves except isolations where their lack of roundness is a problem.

An orange constitutes 1 of your 5 recommended daily portions of fruit and veg.

"Contact Balls"

Some manufacturers produce heavier hard stage balls, which they call "Contact Balls". They're like a training ball for 1 ball Contact with an acrylic. They're no more relevant to multiball than a stage ball.

If you like the feel of this extra weight for 1 ball Contact, then these are for you. Very few professional Contact performers use them, even for training, favouring instead acrylics and soft stage balls.

Balls Not Recommended for Multiball Contact

Balls that are heavy and so risk causing problems with wrist or finger damage like RSI (repetitive strain injury) are not recommended for Contact.

This includes: Lucite Balls, (real) crystal balls, stone balls and solid steel ball bearings.

It is the weight of the balls that is the issue, so for example if you were wishing to palmspin 2 small (50mm) crystal or stone balls in one hand, this is unlikely to be a problem. But If you palmspin with 2 larger (75mm) crystal or stone balls, you are heading for trouble. Consider them to be strictly ornaments.

Hand to Ball Size Chart For Learning Multiball

To complete the lessons in this book you will need 4 balls - this appendix will help you decide which size balls are suitable for you to start learning Multiball Contact with.

Measure your hand as shown opposite and then use the chart on this page should help you decide what size balls to buy. Most ball manipulators use 70 - 75mm (2 ¾" - 3") diameter acrylics.

Those with very small hands might want to use 65mm (2.5") balls.

Larger balls lead to smoother Contact but can be a little more of an effort to learn with. No matter how large your hands, balls larger than 76.6mm (3") are not recommended for beginners.

Imperial ball sizes   **Metric ball sizes**

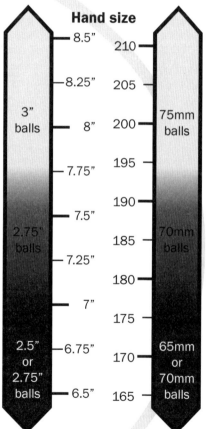

This chart doesn't show the upper limits of what is possible. Highly skilled 190mm hands can perform comfortably with pyramids of 85mm balls, and my 200mm hands can just about spin a pyramid of 100mm acrylic balls, but because of the weight and the strain, this is not sensible. Just 30 seconds will ensure that my hands and wrists are in pain the next day.

Measuring Ball Size

It's very difficult to accurately measure the diameter of a ball, but it can be useful to tell the difference between 3" and 75mm balls, this is the best method:

Wrap a piece of paper around its equator (middle), and mark off the length of the circumference.

Measure this length with a ruler and divide it by Pi (π=3.142). For example:

1) If the circumference is 235.6mm then 235.6 / 3.142 = 75mm diameter ball.

2) In inches you measure 9.42" (239.4mm) then 9.42 / 3.142 = 3" (76.6mm) diameter.

Common Ball Sizes

Measuring Hand Size

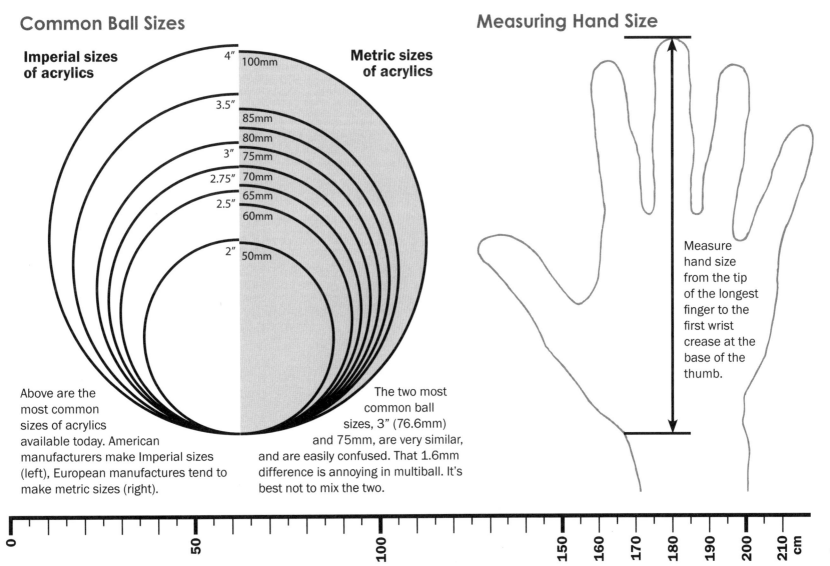

Imperial sizes of acrylics

4" 100mm
3.5"
85mm
80mm
3" 75mm
2.75" 70mm
65mm
2.5" 60mm
2" 50mm

Metric sizes of acrylics

Above are the most common sizes of acrylics available today. American manufacturers make Imperial sizes (left), European manufactures tend to make metric sizes (right).

The two most common ball sizes, 3" (76.6mm) and 75mm, are very similar, and are easily confused. That 1.6mm difference is annoying in multiball. It's best not to mix the two.

Measure hand size from the tip of the longest finger to the first wrist crease at the base of the thumb.

0   50   100   150 160 170 180 190 200 210 cm

Big Balls

Larger balls have the advantages that they are more smooth, stable and far more visual. The disadvantages of larger balls are that they are more expensive, feel **huge** when you start working with them, and the extra weight can put more strain on your wrists and fingers.

Some more experienced multiball manipulators have upgraded in size and weight from standard 3" acrylics to larger 80mm or even 85mm. This makes 8 ball Contact look fantastic, super big and super slow, but the extra strain and weight can cause a few problems. And can be limiting when it comes to 9, 10 and 11 ball manipulation.

Cost of Acrylics

The cost of acrylic balls varies with size. The following is an estimate of 2006 prices:

70mm or 2.75":
  o Cost £20, €22 or US$25 each ball
75mm or 3":
  o Cost £25, €34 or US$28-35 each ball
100mm or 4":
  o Cost £45 - £60, €69 - 82 or US$85 each ball!

Small Balls

Small balls are cheaper, and tend to visually disappear into the hands, they are generally lighter and more skittish (less stable) than larger balls.

Some manipulators find slightly smaller balls can be an advantage for the first month or so of learning palmspinning. After that, they often wish to change up to larger balls.

I use 50mm (2") acrylics to practise palmspinning 7 balls in one hand. Balls this small are not very smooth or stable. Generally I don't practise with less than 5 of them in each hand.

Smaller balls are also popular for combining magic with Contact, as they can be palmed more easily ("palming" is a magic technique used to make objects appear and disappear).

What is Difficulty?

In manipulation, difficulty is a measure of the degree of control required to do a move; how difficult it is to **do.**

Difficulty is also a measure of the amount of practice time required to gain that level of control, how difficult it is to **learn.**

It's quite bizarre this difficulty thing. Take walking as an example - you do it everyday, and you wouldn't say it's difficult, but then look at how many hours' effort a baby puts into learning to walk! For most people walking is very easy to do, but very difficult to learn.

If you look at it from a learning point of view, then "difficult" moves (like palmspinning pyramids) are easier to learn than walking.

With most moves in Contact, once you can do them, you can do them (although you might get a bit rusty without regular practice). With time, you forget the hours weeks and months spent practising, and all the moves feel relaxing and easy to do.

There's No Such Thing as a Natural!

Well OK, there is a little bit of natural variation, but not very much! Two main factors determine how easily you can learn Contact:

○ Previous experience of similar arts and
○ Training methods and a good teacher

Previous experience of similar arts

The more experience you have had with similar fine motor control activities such as other forms of manipulation, martial arts, dancing, poi, juggling, magic and many sports, the easier it is to learn another one - like Contact.

Whenever I teach someone who seems to learn Contact very easily, I ask them, "Have you done any dance or martial art?" and every single time I get an answer like "Oh yeah, I did 5 years of Tai Chi" or "I used to do dance classes when I was younger", or i find out they are a musician. In doing these other activities, they have learnt a lot of physical control and coordination, and those are pure Contact skills.

If you haven't done anything like this before, great, here's your chance to start refining those fine motor skills, and let the ball act like a little Yoda, teaching you how to move with better and finer control. These skills will also help you learn all kinds of movement, dance, martial arts and manipulation with other props.

Training methods and a good teacher

Learning how to learn is a very useful thing. It's a skill that can be taught, improved, refined and practised.

Improving your training methods will make your training more effective, and your learning easier. See page 77 in the Lessons section for some tips on training methods.

The best way to learn a physical skill is the way boxers do it, get a coach. There's nothing better than being taught one-to-one or in small groups by a very experienced teacher. You can tap into their experience of how to do the trick, and their experience of how to learn Contact the most painless way.

What about Genes?

There is a suggestion that somehow someone is a "natural" Contact Juggler implying that there is something in their genes which makes them better at playing with balls.

This is the whole nature vs nurture debate, and yes, there must be some element of genetic make up that determines how easily a particular person learns Contact. For example left handers are generally more clumsy in life, but have a far higher success rate in sports that require co-ordination and use of both sides of the brain. Whether this is innate (at birth), or as a result of lefties having to use both sides of the brain more, due to living in a right handed world is not yet known.

But observation of other manipulators suggests that genetic differences play a **very** minor role in how easily a particular person learns Contact.

From personal experience, given the difficulty I had learning the basics, if there is such a thing as a natural, I'm certainly not one. A quick chat with some of the most highly skilled professional contact juggler in the world, suggests that they certainly aren't either.

To summarise, if someone is learning Contact "quickly" it is probably because of one of the following:

- They've practised activities already which give them good control
- They're very practised at learning
- They have a very good teacher
- They aren't actually learning quickly - they have lower standards of quality in their moves giving a false perception of progress.

Formations in the inspiration section have numbers next to their titles eg:

"Hourglass [3.1.3]"

This is Morphing Notation, a useful and slightly geeky method for describing shapes of formations.

It won't make you better at Contact, but if you start exploring formations and morphing, you will find that there are dozens of them that are not described in this book. You may find this notation useful in recording those you find.

The basic idea of morphing notation is to list the number of balls in each layer, starting at the bottom. For example a 4 ball pyramid is [3.1] as shown below. It's written in square brackets just to make it clear that it is morphing notation.

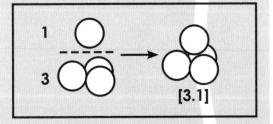
[3.1]

Punctuation

In written text, punctuation tells you the spacing between words. In Morphing Notation, punctuation indicates the separation (between the ball centres) of each layer of balls.

- "**.**" Full stop – normal spacing, like in a pyramid, about 50-80% of a ball diameter between the layers.
- "**-**" Dash – bigger than a full stop. The layers are 1 ball diameter apart.
- "**,**" Comma – smaller spacing than a full stop between the layers.

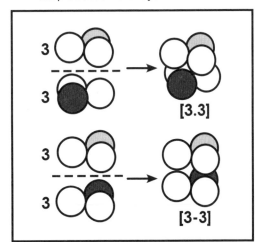

Punctuation differentiates between these two configurations of [3 3]

Orientation

Usually formations are notated in layers from bottom to top. Some formations are much clearer if described left to right [LR] eg:

[LR 1.3.1.3.1] Is the 9 ball Torpedo below.

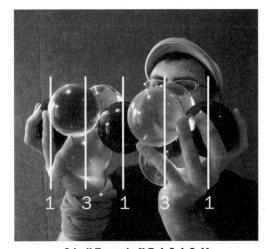

9 ball Torpedo [LR 1.3.1.3.1]
For clarity here the black balls are the 1's.

149

Some formations are easier to notate front to back or even diagonally.

A good example is the 7 ball flower [1.5.1] (below) which can be turned in all directions. It's more convenient to note the change in orientation than to try to change the numbers.

Another example, the 10 ball staircase is easier to notate as the diagonal: Staircase [Diag 2.2.2.2.2]

One formation in one position can often be notated from many different directions. This Staircase could also be written:
- Bottom to top [1.4.4.1],
- Left to right [LR 1.4.4.1], or even
- Front to back [FB 2.6.2].

But these are ambiguous, the 4.4 layers can be in many positions, and a 6 could be many shapes! Choose the simplest orientation to notate your formations.

Commas and Demons

Commas, the smallest spacing between layers, don't appear very frequently in formations. A critical place is the 8 ball demons on page 121 and shown in the box right.

A Celestial Demon without the bottom ball would form a 7 ball formation the crown [3,3,1].

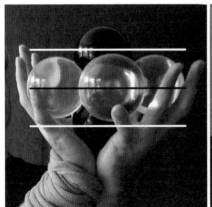
Flower [1.5.1]

Flower [LR 1.5.1]

Flower [FB 1.5.1]

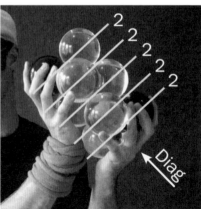
2 balls are hidden at the back of the Staircase [Diag 2.2.2.2.2]

Layer Configuration

[1.3.3.1]   [1.3-3.1]

[1.3,3,1]
Celestial
Demon

Punctuation differentiates between these 3 configurations

S ometimes it is helpful to specify the shape of the balls within a layer. 3 balls are usually arranged in a triangle, or sometimes a line:

4 balls are usually assumed to be in a square unless noted otherwise, (e.g. diamond or line). Ball layers are arranged either on a square grid, or a triangular grid.

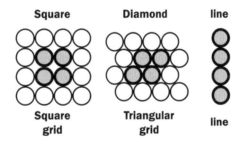

Square	Diamond	line
Square grid	Triangular grid	line

5, 6 and 7 have many more options. The 5 ball ring is one of the few arrangements where the balls do not fit neatly onto the square or triangular grids.

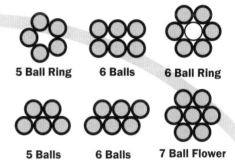

5 Ball Ring	6 Balls	6 Ball Ring
5 Balls	6 Balls	7 Ball Flower

Usually the most stable arrangement is that which has the balls most in contact with each other. If nothing is specified then choose the prettiest arrangement!

The arrangements and packing of spheres is a subject much studied in science, engineering and mathematics. It is used to understand the arrangement of atoms in crystals. You may gain inspiration for your multiball formations by studying a little of this. A good place to start would be to search with these keywords: "Face centred cubic", "Crystal lattice structures" and "Hexagonal close packing".

Appendix 5: Names & "Ownership" of Moves

Until I started this book, most multiball moves didn't have any name. They were called "this one" or "that one with 8 balls". To add to the confusion, other moves are referred to by several different names, given to them by contact jugglers who have independently developed them.

In a book, calling all the moves "this one" is not practical. So I've tried to give the moves and families in this book some names that make sense, or use the most common existing name.

Who Invented What?

Often in Contact I see that someone claims to have "invented a move" which I had considered to be part of the tradition of manipulation and know to have existed even before they started Contact. This doesn't mean that they didn't put the effort in and independently develop it for themselves, but that they weren't the first to do it.

I've specifically chosen not to attach credit to people who claim to have invented tricks, including not crediting moves, concepts and teaching methods that I've developed or played a part in developing. This is because I'm not sure that this accreditation can be done accurately. Much of Contact in the last 20 years has been an oral tradition, with little written down or recorded on video.

An exception to this is that I've chosen to credit Michael Moschen for his outstanding contribution to manipulation and Contact - see Appendix 6.

A spiritual and talented contact juggler Mr Om once said on this subject, "We are too small for creation", he was implying that nothing we can do is more than a speck in comparison to the creation of the universe.

Copyright & Ownership of Moves

We cannot own moves. We cannot copyright or patent a movement in dancing or juggling - and a good thing too!

So if you believe that you have created a move and you don't want anyone else to copy that move, then keep it secret, don't show it to anyone and very soon you will see someone else develop it independently. We cannot own moves.

We can own routines. It is possible to legally copyright a routine or a choreography (and it is a sensible thing to do too). A routine is a very personal thing that takes a long time to develop. It is never good to copy someone else's routine without permission.

Don't copy routines, create your own. When you are creating your own routine, don't even copy little sections from existing performances and routines, create your own sequences.

No Secrets Here, We're Not the Magic Circle

There is no need to keep secrets in Contact. There is no trick to Contact, no magnets, no wires, no secret which if revealed "explains" how it is done and spoils the effect. There are only techniques that can help you to learn to do it better.

It is true that Contact has many close ties with magic. An acrylic can be seen as a "magic" crystal ball as used by fortune tellers to see into the future. Moves and concepts such as isolations and other "illusion based Contact", create magical effects and Ball Contact can be used effectively in magic performances. But because it lacks the element of deception that is usually associated with magic, Contact is usually considered to be manipulation rather than magic.

Pay it Forward

The philosophy amongst the European manipulators that I train with is that the more you share and teach, the more will come back to you.

Create your moves, share them with others. Let them grow and develop and later they will come back to you with many variations and new ideas to play with.

Manipulation is an open source community. Pay it forward, that is the Contact way. "Pay it forward" as a concept in manipulation means that if someone teaches you a move, or helps you with some technique, then instead of trying to repay them, which is often difficult, and the teacher usually has more experience than you, "Pay it forward" by teaching it to three other people. In the long term this helps the whole Contact community (It's also nice to say thank you, and cake can be used as a good alternative to "pay it forward").

Pre-History of Contact

Balls have been played with in many cultures around the world for thousands of years. Historically several things were united to form the origins of modern Contact:

- Chinese medicine ball palmspinning
- General manipulation and magic
- 1 ball body rolling
- Object Balancing

Chinese medicine ball Palmspinning

A technique with strong Oriental origins is palmspinning with small metal Chinese medicine balls, also known as "Baoding balls". This is the ancestor of Multiball Contact techniques and can be traced back to the Ming Dynasty (1368-1644).

General manipulation and magic

Forms of dance and manipulation take influences from each other. There has been manipulation, juggling and magic for thousands of years, with many different props, these techniques have influenced ball Contact.

For example the famous billiard ball manipulation routine from the magician Cardini in the mid-20th Century and the fundamental concept of "isolation" has existed in belly dancing for millennia.

In the 1970s and 80s several manipulators and jugglers were independently developing what was later to become Ball Contact.

Notable amongst them was Tony Duncan, who in summer 1978 developed moves incorporating "forearm rolls" and "half butterflies" (half of the 1 ball "butterfly" movement) into juggling and in 1983 and had a 1 ball routine of "Dynamic Balancing" (the name he prefers "Contact Juggling"). With Multiball, he was working on 3 ball separated palm rolling cascades in 1980. His pioneering Contact was later to be eclipsed by that of Michael Moschen.

1 ball body rolling

This has origins in Asia using a woven basket ball (see Chinlone right). It came to the West in the 1800s, brought by highly skilled "oriental jugglers" who inspired incredible body rollers including; Paul Cinquevalli (1859-1918), Enrico Rastelli (1896-1931) and Francis Brunn (1922/3-2004).

Today, some of the best body rolling skills can be seen in Rhythmic Gymnastics, which has existed since the 1880s and has been an Olympic sport since 1984.

Chinlone

The national sport of Myanmar is Chinlone, a team or solo game much like a form of hacky sack played with a woven wicker ball. Variations exist across Southeast Asia under many names: Takraw, Sepak Raga, Sipa, Kator and Da Cau.

The origins of these may be related to the ancient Chinese game of Cuju or Tsu Chu (200BC), considered to be the earliest form of football. This split in the 8th and 9th centuries into two threads; the well known thread being the regulated competitive team sport - football, and the other thread, co-operative team and solo sports and games, like Chinlone, hacky sack and perhaps Contact.

"To play Chinlone well, the whole team must be absolutely in the moment – their minds cannot wander or the ball will drop, players experience an intensely focused state of mind, similar to that achieved in Zen meditation, which they refer to as jhana."
- "Chinlone" in Wikipedia

Michael Moschen

Michael Moschen is a conceptual artist, of manipulation and juggling, who performs with a wide range of objects to create spectacles of intense beauty.

Moschen played a key roll in developing modern Ball Contact with his routine "*Light*" about life and death, in 1985. It is still available to buy on video (*Great performances In Motion: with Michael Moschen, 1991*).

After two decades, *Light* has stood the test of time well. It is a beautiful and mesmerising routine - recommended viewing for all manipulators. With *Light*, Moschen was the first to use transparent "crystal" balls, to create a performance which combined the existing techniques of 1 ball body rolling, palm rolling, palmspinning, ball manipulation and balance. An artform which would later be called "Contact".

Moschen developed much of the material in *Light*. He appears work in his manipulation not with "moves", but at a higher level, with pure techniques and concepts of movement.

The following are accredited to Moschen:
- Palm Circle Isolations
- Snakes and trains
- 7 ball "Moschen Transfers"
- Isolating 1 ball through 4 ball pyramid manipulations e.g. isolated thumb-lifts
- The Butterfly (a 1 ball move which is not described in this book)

Each of these is a unique concept: not one move but a whole family of moves.

The movie *The Labyrinth* in 1986 was where Crystal Ball Manipulation became famous. Jareth - The Goblin King played by David Bowie plucked a bubble from the air, and performed a few butterflies with it. Later he spun a pyramid of 4 balls. It wasn't Bowie who was manipulating the balls, but Moschen standing behind him. There was very little Contact in the film, but the magical effect created with the balls was etched deeply in people's memories.

Pandora's box had been opened. After watching Labyrinth, the public were fascinated, thousands wanted to learn to manipulate balls and they wanted a name for this new thing...

Contact Juggling

The public wanted a name for this thing, James Ernest gave them "Contact Juggling". The public wanted to know how to do it and Ernest gave them that too, with his book *Contact Juggling* (1990). Ernest paid a great service to ball manipulation by helping to teach and spread the techniques of Contact throughout the world. Now 15 years old, the book is a little dated and out of print, although it is still available to buy.

He defined: "*Contact Juggling: Manipulations of a single Object or Object groups, usually involving very little tossing or spinning. Ex. balls, ball stacks, and some types of stick, hat and plate work...*"
"*Contact Juggling is above all, graceful and absorbing.*" (Contact Juggling, 2nd Ed, 1991, page 2)

It's more accurate to say that he defined Contact Juggling as: "The ball manipulation in his book *Contact Juggling*" rather than ball manipulation in general.

A cynical view from some aspects of the juggling community is that Contact Juggling was James Ernest's name for what Moschen did in the routine "Light". Moschen doesn't use the term Contact Juggling. This led to a disagreement between the two camps, supporters of Moschen and supporters of Ernest, wasting time that could have been better spent playing with balls!

A quick count suggests that 75% of the tricks in the book *Contact Juggling*, were performed in "Light", or other routines by Moschen. But much of Contact Juggling existed before Moschen. Whatever Contact Juggling was then, it has grown much in 20 years and at its cutting edge has evolved far beyond those origins.

Ball Contact

Some who criticised "Contact Juggling" claimed that it was not "Juggling". The author of this book, being both a juggler and a manipulator, agrees that you have to take a very loose definition of "Juggling" to include either the Multiball Contact in this book or much of 1 and 2 ball Contact within a definition of juggling.

But the word Contact is a good one. *Ball Contact* is playing with a ball. So what is *Multiball Contact*? "The stuff that is in this book, and stuff that is like it." It is a kind of Ball Manipulation.

Not Just Balls

Contact with balls is only a small part of the growing world of Manipulation and juggling. Manipulators are working with many different props, and concepts and movements regularly cross pollinate from one prop to another. For example hoop manipulation, contact moves with juggling clubs and Contact Staff.

Recent Trends

Today, all forms of manipulation including Contact are more widespread than they have ever been. Every year they become even more popular and there is an ever increasing level of skill.

The quality of Contact performances, both on stage and on the street is improving too. Worldwide there are some amazing performers. The likes of Jeanine, Bruno, Nika, Emanuele, Pich, Dimitri, Jago, Ryan Mellors, Matt Hennem, Kelvin Kalvus, Mister Crystal, Mika Quartz, Mr Om and Miss Frix to name just a few in Europe.

Recreational Contact, is also booming, for manipulators who put their emphasis on the social side of Contact and play, meditation and dancing, rather than on performance.

The Future of Contact

The future of Contact looks good! There are new moves and new concepts being developed in Contact every year and I expect these developments to continue in directions we are yet to dream of.

Until now the people learning Multiball Contact were pioneers and early adopters. Now, I hope with this book, this information is accessible to all.

Where is Contact Going?

I don't know.
But this kids got potential...
And it's going, wherever you take it.

For a full up-to-date list of links, of new projects, books and videos related to Contact and Manipulation see our website:

www.MinistryofManipulation.com

Here's a few links to get you started:

Chinlone

http://www.chinlone.com/
http://en.wikipedia.org/wiki/Chinlone

Michael Moschen

PBS Great Performances:
In motion: with Michael Moschen
1991 only available on VHS
Labyrinth 1986
Michael Moschen's website:
http://www.michaelmoschen.com

James Ernest

"Contact Juggling" Book
1990 ISBN: 0-9634054-0-3
Now out of print, and perhaps a little out of date. http://www.cheapass.com

Online Contact Forum (English):

http://www.contactjuggling.org

In Isolation DVD

http://www.beard.co.uk/
Produced in 2006 *In Isolation* is the largest concentration of high quality European Contact available to buy on DVD. Multiball Contact is a major focus of the project, and there is a big section of Contact by the Author - Drew Batchelor.

Sphercular Vision DVD

http://www.spherculism.net/
Produced in 2006 *Sphercular vision* is video from the Poi and Staff community which also features some Multiball Contact by Drew and others. *Sphercular vision* features a great soundtrack and editing effects.

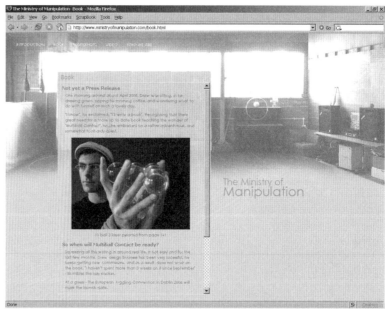

The Ministry of Manipulation

Index By Difficulty

These difficulty ratings use the Super Ultimate Cosmic Contact Pyramids of difficulty scale is explained on page 5.

Multiball Contact
Index By Difficulty

Difficulty 5

Index By Name

With Thanks to

Personal thanks:
Dr Mithi for being lovely. My family for supporting me. Thanks to my house mates for putting up with me while I was writing: Dom, The Hangar Crew; Jet Jensen, Alex and Charlotte, Tina, Bruce and Lorraine, Raphael, Nick, Ryan and Chicken and thanks to Matt Hennem for the beer.

Book Helpers thanks:
Thanks for helping with editing and proof reading the manuscript:
Mithila Shafiq, Clare Palmer (www.Firepoise.com), Coleman Walker, Miranda Keeling, Nika, Pich (www.Maniballe.net) and Ryan Mellors.

Thanks for help with developing the layout and assistance with the covers: Helen Turner (www.hurt-design.co.uk) and Lucy Batchelor (www.lucyjanebatchelor.me.uk)

Thanks for help with the individual page layouts: Coleman Walker

Thanks to Dan Gordon-Levitt for the cover photograph, and Krista Zala for assisting by catching balls as they were washed away.

Contact Juggling Thanks

Big Contact Juggling thanks to all the people who have taught and inspired me over the years.

Early on, *Just Jugglers* at the old Drome: Dimitri Ogden, Doug Torrent, Emanuele (for making isolations into isolations), Karine Friez, Selina, Nika and Matt Hennem, One/Crystal Ball Paul, Miranda, Peachi and Cindy. Plus all of the rest of the old Drome Juggling crowd.

And more recently: Ryan Mellors and Jeanine at the Ministry, Dawn, Denise, Ewan, Dan and Andy for the BCJC, Anna from Hungary, Greg Maldonado and Silver Paul. Thanks also to Coleman for making me think.

Thanks to the European Contact legends for the inspiration: Mr Om, Mister Crystal, Kelvin Kalvus, Miss Frix, Bruno Labouret, Mika Quartz, Pich, Vincent and Dafne.

Thanks to Jago Parfitt for In Isolation, Mushy Pea Steve for Contact staff, John Plastic from Bristol juggling convention for showing me that 6 in one hand is possible.

Thanks also to Tony Duncan, Michael Moschen and James Ernest.

Ifor Gaukroger for introducing me to 1 ball Contact. Beinn Muir for teaching me to juggle 4 and 5 balls and much juggling theory and training techniques.

Finally thanks to all the students at my contact juggling courses for having the faith in me to attend the course, which formed the foundations of this book.

Thanks Guys
Drew

About Drew

I've been manipulating balls for over a decade, ever since I was first shown a butterfly by a juggler. For my first two years, I didn't meet another Contact Juggler.

I learnt the fundamentals of Multiball from Dimitri, Emanuele and Doug at the legendary Just Jugglers Drome Workshops in London, sadly now closed. So my roots are in the European and more specifically London style Contact, which aims to be slow, smooth, clean and controlled. I still aspire to those values and each year get a little bit closer to meeting them.

As well as Ball Contact I also love most forms of manipulation, especially: Contact Staff, regular throwy-droppy juggling with balls and clubs, Poi and Lindy Hop (Contact Juggling with a girl!) and vernacular jazz dance.

For Multiball, I use the standard 3" balls. My hand size is 200mm from wrist crease to tip of longest finger, large, but apparently not even in the biggest 5% of men. In either hand, I can palmspin six 2.5" or seven 2" balls in a flat flower. I have even spun four 4" acrylics. But that was painful, I don't recommend it.

I am certainly not the best at Multiball Contact, and I don't claim to be. I look with awe upon the talents of many of my Contact Juggling friends with whom I have had the privilege to train. I've never been much of a performer, I prefer to teach and develop techniques, concepts, moves and teaching methods. Then I sit back and watch the real performers show me how it is meant to be done.

I wouldn't be considered a "natural" manipulator, dancer or juggler. I'm a slow learner who keeps chipping away, trying to understand a new move and studying the small details in order to learn a bigger trick. This has influence greatly the teaching aspect of this book.

I have learned and developed a lot of training and learning techniques. I use these in my own training and when teaching courses and workshops in Contact and other forms of manipulation and dance. I run workshops in London and at many juggling conventions including: the British, Bristol, London and The European Juggling Convention.

I hope you find this to be a useful guide to the world of Multiball Contact.

Happy Contact.

Drew Batchelor
The Ministry of Manipulation
London, November 2006